D1244368

SHELL GUIDES

edited by JOHN BETJEMAN AND JOHN PIPER

CORNWALL
John Betjeman

DORSET
Michael Pitt-Rivers

THE ISLE OF WIGHT
C. J. Pennethorne Hughes

LINCOLNSHIRE
Henry Thorold and Jack Yates

NORFOLK
Wilhelmine Harrod and C. L. S. Linnell

RUTLAND
W. G. Hoskins

SOUTH-WEST WALES
PEMBROKESHIRE AND CARMARTHENSHIRE
Vyvyan Rees

SUFFOLK
Norman Scarfe

WORCESTERSHIRE
James Lees-Milne

---

edited by JOHN PIPER

ESSEX
Norman Scarfe

GLOUCESTERSHIRE
David Verey

KENT
C. J. Pennethorne Hughes

LEICESTERSHIRE
W. G. Hoskins

NORTHUMBERLAND
Thomas Sharp

WILTSHIRE
J. H. Cheetham and John Piper

NORTHAMPTONSHIRE
Juliet Smith

THE SHELL PILOT TO THE SOUTH COAST HARBOURS
K. Adlard Coles

A Shell Guide

Gloucestershire

RESPONSIBILITY IS TO KEEP THE ABILITY TO RESPOND
Robert Duncan

A Shell Guide

Gloucestershire

by David Verey

Faber & Faber London

First published in 1951
by Faber and Faber Limited
24 Russell Square London WC1
Second edition 1970
Printed in Great Britain by
Shenval Press, London and Harlow
All rights reserved

ISBN 0 571 04710 6

Although sponsoring this book, Shell-Mex
and B.P. Ltd would point out that the author
is expressing his own views

© 1970 by Shell-Mex and B.P. Ltd

Illustrations

Front endpaper
The Severn from above
Newnham
Peter Burton

Frontispiece
The Devil from the Last Judge-
ment window, Fairford. From
English Stained Glass, John
Baker and Alfred Lammer,
published by Thames &
Hudson, London

Title page
Roundhouse on The Thames
and Severn canal, Chalford
Edward Piper

Page
7 Deerhurst, Saxon details
Peter Burton

8 Aldsworth
Edward Piper

8 Winson
Edward Piper

8 Sherborne
Edward Piper

8 Little Barrington
Edward Piper

10 Winstone
Edward Piper

10 Aldsworth
Edwin Smith

10 Winson
Edward Piper

11 Tetbury, stone tiles
Peter Burton

12 Chalford, mill
Edward Piper

12 Nailsworth, mill
Edward Piper

14 The Wye at Symond's Yat
Peter Burton

15 The Scowles, Forest of Dean
G. D. Bolton

17 Severn Bridge
Edward Piper

18 Towards the Severn from
Nympsfield
Edwin Smith

19 Orchards from Elmore Back
Edward Piper

20 Elkstone, Norman tympanum
John Piper

Page
20 Quenington, Norman
tympanum
John Piper

21 Rendcomb, Norman font
Peter Burton

22 Chipping Campden
Edward Piper

23 Northleach
Edward Piper

24 Yate
Edward Piper

25 Cirencester from church tower
G. D. Bolton

26 Chipping Campden, Grevel's
House
Peter Burton

28 Snowshill Manor
Peter Burton

29 Stanway House
Christopher Dalton

30 Dyrham Park
Edward Piper

35 Coates, tunnel, east entrance
Edward Piper

37 Gloucester Cathedral
Edward II
Edwin Smith

38 Sapperton, Poole monument
Edward Piper

43 Ashleworth, barn
Edward Piper

43 Ablington, barn
Edwin Smith

44 Avening
Edward Piper

47 Great Barrington, monument
Peter Burton

48 Berkeley Castle
Edward Piper

49 Bibury, Arlington Mill
Edward Piper

50 Bisley, Nether Lypiatt Manor
Davina Verey

51 Bledington
Christopher Dalton

52 Chalford
Edward Piper

53 Cheltenham
G. D. Bolton

Page
54 Cheltenham, Priory Street
John Piper

55 Cheltenham, Lansdown Place
Edward Piper

56 Cheltenham, Bayshill Road
Edward Piper

57 Cheltenham, the Promenade
Edward Piper

58 Cheltenham, Queens Parade
and Christchurch
Edward Piper

59 Cheltenham, Suffolk Square
John Piper

60 Cheltenham
Number 3, Suffolk Square
John Piper

61 Cheltenham
Montpellier Walk
John Piper

62 Cherington
Edward Piper

62 Nagshead
Edward Piper

64 Chipping Campden
Market Hall
Peter Burton

65 Chipping Campden
Almshouses
Peter Burton

66 Chipping Campden
High Street
Edward Piper

66 Chipping Campden
Great House Lodges
Edward Piper

67 Broad Campden Church
Davina Verey

68 Cirencester
Edward Piper

69 Cirencester Park
Edwin Smith

70 Daglingworth, Crucifixion
John Piper

71 Didbrook, cottage
Edwin Smith

72 Dodington
Edward Piper

73 Duntisbourne Rouse
Christopher Dalton

74 Dursley, Market House
Edwin Smith

75 Dursley
Edwin Smith

76 Elkstone
Peter Burton

77 Fairford
Christopher Dalton

78 Frampton Court
orangery and canal
Edward Piper

79 Frampton Court
Edward Piper

80 Gloucester, dock warehouses
Edward Piper

80 Gloucester, west approach
Edward Piper

82 Gloucester Cathedral, choir
Edwin Smith

82 Gloucester Cathedral, cloisters
Peter Burton

84 Gloucester Cathedral
Peter Burton

85 Gloucester, Lanthony Priory
Edward Piper

85 Gloucester, The New Inn
Edwin Smith

86 Hidcote
Edwin Smith

87 Hidcote
Edwin Smith

88 Highnam Lodge
Christopher Dalton

89 Highnam Church
Christopher Dalton

91 Iron Acton Court
Edward Piper

92 Kempley
John Piper

93 Lechlade
National Monuments Record

93 Leonard Stanley
Edward Piper

94 Nailsworth
Peter Burton

95 Newnham from Arlingham
Warth
Edward Piper

96 North Cerney, Manticore
Reece Winstone

97 North Cerney, churchyard
Edward Piper

98 Northleach
Edward Piper

99 Northleach church, nave
Peter Burton

100 Owlpen
Edward Piper

101 Oddington
Christopher Dalton

102 Painswick churchyard
Peter Burton

103 Sapperton, Daneway
Edwin Smith

104 Sezincote
Edwin Smith

105 Sharpness
Edward Piper

106 Stanway House
Christopher Dalton

107 Tetbury Market House
Edwin Smith

108 Tetbury
Edward Piper

109 Tetbury church
Edward Piper

110 Tewkesbury Abbey
Peter Burton

112 Tewkesbury Abbey
Peter Burton

113 Tewkesbury Abbey
Peter Burton

114 Toddington
Peter Burton

115 Upleadon
Edward Piper

116 Little Washbourne
Christopher Dalton

117 Westonbirt Arboretum
Edward Piper

118 at Willersey
Edwin Smith

120 Clifton Suspension Bridge
Edward Piper

120 Bristol, floating harbour and
Cathedral
Edward Piper

122 St Mary Redcliffe, detail
Edward Piper

123 St Mary Redcliffe
Edward Piper

124 Bristol, Dowry Square
Edward Piper

125 Bristol, Temple Church
Edward Piper

126 Windsor Terrace
Edward Piper

127 Royal York Crescent
Edward Piper

128 Blaise Hamlet
Edward Piper

129 Bristol country
Edward Piper

Back endpaper
Barn near Tetbury
Peter Burton

Preface

This book is about Gloucestershire; but I was also asked to include a token description of Bristol. I am indebted to Miss Elizabeth Ralph, FSA, Hon General Secretary of the Bristol and Gloucestershire Archaeological Society, and to the many others who bravely fight for the conservation of our heritage; and most especially to Miss Ethel Stallard of Arlington Mill. I would also pay tribute to the valiant work of the preservation societies; the Council for the Care of Churches, the Society for the Protection of Ancient Buildings, the Victorian Society, the National Trust, the Gloucestershire Branch of the Council for the Preservation of Rural England, the Cirencester Civic Society, and the Period Cottage Improvement Society founded by the late Colonel E. A. Airy and Mrs Airy.

David Verey

Introduction

When the shire of Gloucester was formed in Saxon times, it was and still is without natural or geographical boundaries, and comprises at least three different kinds of landscape of hill, vale and forest. The area is decisively divided by the broad river Severn with a towering escarpment fifty miles long on one side. On top of the escarpment is a rolling plateau dipping gently to the east; known as the Cotswolds it is now designated as an Area of Outstanding Natural Beauty. The western edge is formed by the escarpment, which rises steeply and dramatically from the Severn Vale to around 1,000 feet above sea level in a few places, and stretches from Chipping Campden in the north to Landsdown Hill, near Bath, in the south.

For centuries the whole of the uplands remained open sheep-walks—that tract of "high wild hills and rough uneven ways", complained of by Shakespeare's Earl of Northumberland on his way to Berkeley Castle, and criticized, after inclosure, in a still severer way by another traveller. On leaving Cirencester, Cobbett says: "I came up hill into a country, apparently formerly a down or common, but now divided into large fields by stone walls. Anything so ugly I have never seen before." After ten miles, "all of a sudden", he says, "I looked down from the top of a high hill into the Vale of Gloucester. Never was there, surely, such a contrast in this world. This hill is called Birdlip. . . . All below is fine . . ." From the escarpment there are indeed spectacular views across the Severn Vale to the Forest of Dean and Malvern Hills, which can now be enjoyed from many open spaces available to the public, such as Cleeve Common, Frocester Hill, Stinchcombe Hill, Painswick Beacon, Minchinhampton Common, Dover's Hill, and especially from Haresfield Beacon owned by the National Trust. Westward from here, in the middle distance the Severn makes a vast loop round Arlingham, and then broadens out as the tidal water flows down to pass under the new bridge and meet the Wye at Chepstow. Beyond it rise the wooded scarps of Old Red Sandstone which form the eastern edges of the Forest of Dean. In the foreground, 700 feet below, lies the Vale of Berkeley with its old timber-framed dairy-farms and orchards extending into the Vale of Gloucester further to the north, and the Bristol quarter to the south. From Haresfield we have a bird's-eye view of the three landscapes, Forest, Vale and Wold.

The Cotswold escarpment is the western edge of a limestone plateau which merges gradually into the clay plains of Oxfordshire, leaving outliers in the vales such as Robins Wood Hill and Churchdown. The limestone is composed of small rounded grains of calcium carbonate packed together like the roe of a fish. From this resemblance the stone is called oolite, meaning eggstone. The Inferior Oolite, so called because it is the lower and older stratum of this limestone, is tilted upwards at its western edge. Further east it dips under the Great Oolite which provides finegrained stone, or freestone, which can be carved easily. Some beds provide thin layers of rock which can be split by exposure to frost, thus producing the stone tiles which have always till now been used for roofing. The earliest examples of the use of oolitic tilestones are in the Neolithic long-barrows at Hetty Pegler's Tump, near Uley, and Belas Knap, Sudeley. The Romans used tilestones for roofing their buildings and they gave them pointed ends. Medieval examples are said to be found in places like Chipping Campden. They are carefully graduated, and the huge stone tiles at the bottom of the roofs require enormous

ALDSWORTH
WINSON
SHERBORNE
LITTLE BARRINGTON

p. 10 WINSTONE, ALDSWORTH, WINSON
p. 11 Stone tiles near TETBURY

oak beams to support them. Their weight is one of the reasons for the decline of this industry. In 1969 no quarry in Gloucestershire is producing stone tiles, and the traditionalist has to resort to cannibalization. Second-hand stone tiles are carefully preserved by builders, and fetch a high price. Generally most stone quarries are now deserted, stone having become a luxury building material. The best of all the deserted quarries is that at Leckhampton. It was opened in 1793 and provided the beautifully dressed stone for the building of Regency Cheltenham. It is now a spectacular cliff on the escarpment edge above the town.

There is no doubt that much of the beauty of the Cotswolds is derived from its old stone buildings. The oolitic limestones can shade from yellow and cream to brown. Guiting stone, still quarried at Coscombe, is a deep yellow, and was used in such well-known buildings as Stanway House and G. E. Street's church at Toddington. These buildings achieve a visual accord with the landscape, and if Cobbett had had a mind to penetrate into the many delicious valleys of the Cotswold rivers, Churn, Coln, Windrush or Leach, he would have found much to delight him. Even the barns, however, on the high wolds are of outstanding quality, and every effort is and should be made to preserve this district. The local people regard it highly, even jealously; it is an extremely popular farming area, where £300 is gladly paid per acre for a somewhat thin soil, though barley and sheep do well enough.

Although the Stroud Valleys are excluded from the Area of Outstanding Natural Beauty they are physically a part of the Cotswolds. The escarpment has been cut into by the river Frome and its tributaries, producing a number of deep valleys some thickly wooded, while others like the Golden Valley and Nailsworth Valley are the scene of early industrial development. The cloth for which Stroud had become famous was superfine broadcloth, a high-quality fabric. After fulling, the warp and weft of the cloth were in-

visible. If it was dyed in Gloucestershire it was usually done after fulling, and Stroudwater reds were famous as early as the fifteenth century. In the following century Leland describes also Thornbury, Wickwar, Wotton-under-Edge, Alderley, and Dursley, as pretty clothing towns. The best mills in the Stroud area to survive are St Mary's, Chalford, Dunkirk and Egypt at Nailsworth, Stanley Mills, Lodgemore, and Ebley Mills, which were surprisingly enlarged by that High Church architect, G. F. Bodley.

The Forest of Dean lies between the rivers Severn and Wye and includes the Dean Forest Park which was designated in 1938 as the first National Forest Park in England and Wales. The scenery is spectacular, varying from dense coniferous forest to open oak woods, and from deep wooded valleys to high ridges giving long views. Most of the land of the Park is owned and run by the Forestry Commission, whose efforts to combine productive forestry with a high degree of public access appears to be entirely successful. A circular motor route is proposed, using existing roads, linking the beauty spots and including some of the most attractive parts of the forest, such as Cannop Ponds and Upper Soudley Ponds. The Severn Bridge will enable many more people to come to the Dean, and see this extraordinary forest and its culminating feature, the fantastic ravine of the looping Wye at Symond's Yat.

Symond's Yat has been a strategic point from earliest times, and the camp which lies inside the entrenchments probably dates from 450 B.C. Later, it formed part of Offa's Dyke, built c. A.D. 760 to keep out the Welsh. The history of the Forest is ancient. It is one of the few survivors of the old Royal Forests of England, and was excellent for hunting, with the additional attraction of having a wealth of minerals. For nearly two thousand years it has been a source of excellent iron-ore deposits, which are found in pockets of the carboniferous limestone. The coal measures are in the centre, and as these are

Mills at CHALFORD
and NAILSWORTH

p. 14 The Wye at Symond's Yat
p. 15 The Scowles, Roman iron workings
in the Forest of Dean

forested it is the prettiest coalfield imaginable. In the fourteenth century the iron trade was prospering, partly due to the demand for iron consequent on the wars, and partly to the sale of agricultural implements at Gloucester Fair. We know what a Forest miner then looked like from the Freeminer's brass at Newland. He wears a cap, a thick flannel jacket and leather breeches tied below the knee and carries a wooden hod on his back and holds a candlestick, like a pipe, between his teeth. It became necessary for an Act of Parliament in 1838 to redefine the qualifications necessary to become a Freeminer. He had to be a male of twenty-one years, or older, born within the Hundred of St Briavels, and one who had worked for a year and a day in mines in that hundred. Only Freeminers were allowed to work coal or iron; but they were allowed to sell or rent the portions of land alloted to them, and this eventually led to companies coming in, and far greater productivity. However, these industries have not survived the Second World War, and the emphasis is now entirely on forestry.

Over the years oak woods have predominated and provided suitable timber for the ship-building industry. It is said that the Spanish Armada was instructed to destroy the Forest if nothing else in England. The use of the heavy branches of open grown oak for the timbers of wooden ships persisted until the middle of the nineteenth century. Since then the demand for softwood from coniferous trees has grown rapidly and resulted in the gradual felling of the oakwoods, and their replanting with conifers and mixtures of conifers and hardwoods. The Forest's present area is 24,000 acres. The old-established villages of the Dean are all on the perimeter, and so there is a ring of medieval churches. The churches inside the Forest are all nineteenth century, built to serve the later industrial population. The area is a plateau of which the rim is formed by resistant old red sandstone. Within it three lofty ridges, each running almost due north and south, break up the surface with such effect that it would be hard to find a level part of more than 200 acres. The syncline is composed of three series of rocks, the old red sandstone outer ring, massive carboniferous limestones, followed by the central part of the saucer filled with coal measures, sandstones and shales. The old red sandstone (Devonian) is a good building stone. The limestones, blue-grey to buff, give rise to the magnificent scenery of the Wye gorge at Symond's Yat and at Chepstow. The tough quartz conglomerate from the Devonian rocks made excellent millstones for both cider and grain grown in the neighbouring vales. The best stone produced today is called pennant sandstone, found in the coal measures series. It has a great range of colour, from blue-grey to yellow, and Bixhead Quarries, near Cannop Ponds, are kept busy.

The clay Vales of Gloucester, Berkeley and the Severn have a foundation of the softer rocks of the Trias and Lower Jurassic. It is the blue lias clay which dominates. It is often more than 700 feet thick, and is pre-eminently pasture land. It also has its economic uses for bricks and tiles. Although the clay lowlands suffer from excessive dampness in winter, in places there are patches of superficial sand deposits which gave the early Saxon settlers dry sites for their villages, e.g. Twyning and Cheltenham. The general name for the interglacial deposit is Cheltenham sands. The area of vale north-east of the Dean is centred on Newent, and is still a deeply rural district. The better-known vale on the west side of the Severn has always been dairy country famous in the past for its Double Gloucester cheeses. Both are fruit growing. This was a far richer country than the Cotswolds. Fat cattle in the Vale compared more than favourably with the almost wild sheep on the wolds. There must still be many medieval timber-framed buildings in the Vale, besides the great establishments of the nobility like the castles of Berkeley and Thornbury. Country houses are at Frampton, Hardwicke and Forthampton. Socially, too, it was more desirable, though this trend has for long been reversed in favour of the more accessible Cotswolds, luckily however still outside the commuter belt. The Severn Bridge and motorways should now even it up.

The Severn Bridge, 1966

Towards the Severn from Nympsfield

The river itself has not added much to the amenities of the Vale owing to its tides and dangerous currents. It was probably more navigable in the reign of the first Elizabeth. The Severn Wildfowl Trust at Slimbridge has however provided a great interest for many people, as well as being of considerable scientific importance, for the research work covers all aspects of wildfowl biology. Science too has changed the appearance of the estuary with its two great atomic power stations, at Berkeley and Oldbury. The Severn can take innovation; here was the first iron bridge, the launching of the first iron boat, and the first wireless transmission across water. Old and new go hand in hand in the ancient manor of Berkeley. "There was a castle," wrote V. Sackville-West, "sullen, secretive, it looked and still looks across the bright green water-meadows where sea-gulls circle and wild geese fly. Nothing but its colour and its beauty could save it from being wholly sinister. Edward II died there in 1327 after five months' imprisonment. Dark tales but Berkeley is not dark. It

is rose red and grey, red sandstone and grey (tufa) limestone, the colour of old brocade . . . the coats of its hunt servants not pink but canary yellow. . . ." Gone are the days when the Earl of Berkeley could hunt his hounds the whole way from the Severn to Berkeley Square without riding over anyone else's land; but the Berkeley family still reigns in Berkeley Castle, and could no doubt still provide a lamprey or a salmon for Buckingham Palace if the occasion required.

The history of the Cotswolds was for many centuries connected with that of the wool trade. The wide sheep pastures, the fullers' earth in the soil, the plentiful streams, and the network of Roman roads were all contributing factors. It is natural pastoral country with a clean free-draining limestone that grows bone and has carried sheep since Roman times. The principal Roman road junction within the area was at Cirencester where roads from Colchester and London converge on the Fosse Way. By the end

18

of the second century Cirencester was next in size only to London. In the fourth century it became the seat of provincial government. The growth of the town must have been largely dependent on the wealth of the region. Very many villas have been excavated or partly excavated in the neighbourhood; but of their exact economic basis we are still mostly ignorant. Great wealth, however, had accumulated in the hands of a few, enough to provide luxurious houses and a lively school of mosaicists. Several of these villas were still functioning in the fifth century.

Saxon invaders then began to settle in the plains. Deerhurst, situated in the Severn plain, has the most important Saxon remains in the county; but infiltrations into the Cotswolds from the upper Thames valley also occurred and Saxon churches are to be found at Somerford Keynes, the Ampneys, Bibury, Coln Rogers, Daglingworth, Duntisbourne Rouse, Edgeworth, Miserden and Winstone. By the time of the Norman Conquest the whole country had been fairly evenly developed except for the Cotswold scarp, the hills round Bisley and the Forest of Dean. At Cirencester the Saxons built a church as long as any in England with the possible exceptions of York and St Albans, though nothing of it remains above ground. The Saxons were then dispossessed and replaced by Norman lords who instigated a huge programme of church building. The county is one of the richest in respect of surviving Norman architecture, with a hundred churches still essentially Norman. By 1082 the first wool merchants' guild in England was started at Burford just over the county boundary, and Flemish weavers came to England in the wake of the Conqueror. The wool trade became the backbone of England's economy and

Orchards: across the Severn from Elmore Back, ELMORE

she soon obtained a monopoly over all other European countries.

Several of Gloucestershire's Norman churches retain that rare feature, a stone vaulted chancel, such as at Hampnett, Rudford, Avening, Elkstone and Kempley. At Coln St Dennis there is a pier in each of the corners which once must have supported a vault, and at Blockley there is a three-bay chancel with the preparations for vaulting still visible. Sculptured tympana are to be found among the Cotswold churches at Ampney St Mary, Stratton, Harnhill, Little Barrington, Lower Swell, Eastleach Turville, Elkstone, Quenington and South Cerney. The subject at Elkstone is a Majesty with the Evangelists' emblems, the Agnus Dei, and the Hand of God. The design is unsophisticated when compared with the conventional ornament and the beak-heads on the arch. At Quenington there are two tympana, that on the south doorway, the Coronation of the Virgin, is like the one at Elkstone with vigorous naïve carving filling the space awkwardly. Here too the arch has many beak-heads. In the north tympanum at Quenington the subject of the sculpture is the Harrowing of Hell. The sun disk with a face in it is a very unusual and early feature. The Southrop font is unique in the county and has figure sculpture far in advance of anything else. The font at Rendcomb resembles one in Hereford Cathedral and has figures in an arcade, and a band of Greek key-pattern above.

The thirteenth century was a period of serious border warfare in which the west part of the county suffered, so that more Early English architecture is to be found in the peaceful and prosperous Cotswolds, particularly charming examples surviving at Wyck Rissington and Cherington. Many chancels were lengthened by the clergy as the liturgy became more elaborate. In fact thirty Cotswold churches have notable Early English features; but there are not so many in the rest of the county. However, most of the

Norman carving:

left above: Tympanum, ELKSTONE
left below: North tympanum, QUENINGTON
Right Font, RENDCOMB

early Gothic architecture in Gloucestershire was lost with the destruction of the monasteries. The Decorated period is hardly represented on the Cotswolds at all, except for the usual window insertions of plain character, such as at Little Badminton, plainer still after the Black Death in 1348. However at Minchinhampton and Longborough there are decorated south transepts, and Todenham church was almost wholly rebuilt in the early fourteenth century. The chancel at Meysey Hampton was greatly enriched at this time, but ballflower decoration is usually absent on the hills. We have to go to places in the vale like Badgeworth for that. To find extensive evidence, however, of early fourteenth-century building we must look to Gloucester Cathedral and Tewkesbury Abbey, for the monastic churches were more independent of trade-cycles. The great revival of the wool trade was to coincide with the beginning of Perpendicular architecture.

The Perpendicular style, begun in Gloucester Cathedral as early as 1331–7, went on with little change for 200 years. On the Cotswolds the yields of the wool entirely remodelled great churches like Cirencester, Northleach, Chipping Campden, Fairford, Winchcombe, Lechlade, Chedworth and Rendcomb, and large numbers were given at least Perpendicular towers. Splendid towers were also built in the Bristol quarter at Bitton, Yate, Chipping Sodbury, Thornbury, Abson, Wickwar and Westerleigh. The buttresses of the Gloucestershire towers are set diagonally at the angles, not parallel with the main walls or octagonal as in East Anglia, and the string-courses are usually carried boldly across the buttresses instead of dying out behind them. In the later examples there is an exuberance of surface ornament expressed in almost excessive panelling. The elaborate coronet of Gloucester Cathedral with its pierced battlements and pinnacles was copied at Thornbury and elsewhere. Coates has an early tower, built before

CHIPPING CAMPDEN

1361. Other notable examples are at Coberley, Compton Abdale, Elmstone Hardwicke, Leigh, Kempsford, Oxenton, Gloucester St Nicholas and Wotton-under-Edge. Wool prices reached their highest level in 1480, so that by the time the Tudors came to the throne great private fortunes had been amassed. The monuments to this age, when the Cotswolds stood to Ghent and Bruges as the Australian Bush has in the past century to Bradford, are the churches. Rich wool merchants endowed chantry chapels, many soon to be abolished but not destroyed by the Reformation. The money was the people's and so it was the naves and chapels which were rebuilt, older work surviving in the chancels. The reconstruction of the nave at Cirencester was carried out at the beginning of the sixteenth century by the merchants of the town whose arms and trade marks can be seen carried by carved angels above the great piers of the arcade. The economy of Cirencester was based entirely upon wool from 1300 to 1500. It was a great wool market owned by the Abbot, who charged tolls on every sack of wool sold. For this reason the townsfolk never acquired self-government. The tower was built in *c.* 1400 with money partly provided by Henry IV to show his appreciation of the townspeople's action in putting down the rebellion of Richard II's half-brothers, and partly by the Abbey. This greatest of the "wool" churches was therefore the result of the combined efforts of town and abbey; but the building of other comparable churches such as Northleach, Chipping Campden and Fairford was due entirely to the wool merchants, particularly Fortey, Grevel and Tame, who will for ever be associated with them. These benefactors were fortunate in having stone of superb quality at hand, and master masons to work it. Some unknown genius must have been at work at Northleach and Chipping Campden, a man who made the Perpendicular style into something entirely individual, by his exaggeration of the normal concave or hollow moulding. This

YATE

is particularly apparent in the piers and capitals of the arcades of both these churches. Fairford is best known for its stained glass, all made for the church by Barnard Flower at the time of its rebuilding, *c.* 1500; but the fabric, entirely rebuilt except for the base of the tower, is in the richest late Perpendicular style, and it also contains notable woodwork. On the exterior of the tower are many grotesque sculptures (some from the earlier church) which the medieval mind enjoyed. Emblems of local occupation are also shown, such as the shell of a salt-trader, a hunter's horn and baldric, and of course sheep shears. Sheep shears also appear conspicuously on the tower at Cranham. At Bibury a collection of sheeps' head corbels is preserved in the church, and there are many other examples all over the hills.

The great "wool" churches are mostly situated in small towns of medieval origin, and these have not greatly changed through the ages. Cirencester is of course the largest and has always been so, but it, like the others, entirely escaped development in the nineteenth century. In medieval times the rich woolmen used to farm out the wool and yarn to craftsmen in their homes, where the carding, spinning and weaving were done. The fulling, however, could not be done in the home, so the cloth was brought to the fulling mills. Many of the little towns would have had a fulling mill often combined with the corn mill under one roof. This was so for instance at Arlington Mill, Bibury, in the seventeenth century; but by the middle of the eighteenth century when demand became greater it was found that the waters of the Coln, like other Cotswold streams, were insufficient for what was required. The cloth industry then moved to the Stroud valleys with their better water supply and greater concentration of mills. Although fine broadcloths were still made in Stroud, the area suffered its ups and downs, and was never able to compete with the north of England. The Industrial Revolution therefore passed Gloucestershire by.

This fortunate historical fact has helped to preserve many a delightful townscape intact till now. When the clothiers in Cirencester ceased to prosper at the beginning of the nineteenth century, the town suffered a period of stagnation relieved only by the coaching industry. It is now an agricultural market for the district, supplemented by a few light industries, and the presence of the Royal Agricultural College, founded in the 1850s, brings a bustling life of its own. Architecturally the town has much to offer, with narrow medieval streets lined by gabled Cotswold stone houses jostling with Georgian frontages. These conditions pertain to most of the other smaller Cotswold towns, but in Cirencester the existence of two great private estates almost meeting in the centre of the town has provided it with a unique advantage. Cirencester Park comes right up to the edge of the town with the mansion only a stone's throw from other houses. The planting of the park was done by the first Lord Bathurst at the beginning of the eighteenth century. It is the finest example in England of planting in the pre-landscape manner. Seven rides meet at the first great *rond-point* and ten rides at the Horse Guards, celebrated by Pope in the couplet

Who then shall grace or who improve the soil
Who plants like Bathurst or who builds like Boyle.

Cirencester Park remains inviolate, though the other estate, that of the Abbey, given after the dissolution of the monasteries to the Chester-Master family, is a different story. Green sward still comes right up to the churchyard wall on the north side and will continue to do so; but the sites of the Abbey House (now demolished) and its stables and gardens are being built over with high density housing. This represents the first considerable increase in population in the centre of the town for many years.

At Chipping Campden too there has been considerable post-war building though of a different type. Most of the new houses are privately owned or built by the Council in stone or suitable reconstructed material. The character of the High Street has not altered much since the Campden Trust was formed by F. L. Griggs in 1929. It has buildings of every period from the fourteenth century to the well-designed eighteenth-century

Grevel's House, CHIPPING CAMPDEN

27

houses which give it its peaceful dignity. The only house in the Cotswolds known to have belonged to one of the famous wool merchants is Grevel's house in this street. He died in 1401. In 1610 Sir Baptist Hicks bought the manor and made many gifts to both church and town. Adjacent to the south entrance to the churchyard stand the Jacobean lodges and gateway of the old manor of Campden built by Hicks but destroyed in the Civil War. Two pavilions at either end of a former terrace survive. They are of ashlar with Renaissance motifs and twisted chimney stacks. These buildings show a style far more advanced than the local vernacular and reflect Sir Baptist's London connections. Opposite are his Almshouses, vernacular perhaps and hardly touched by the Renaissance, but symmetrical and stylish on the plan of the letter "I" for King James.

Northleach has no great house, but its magnificent church shows what kind of a man Fortey was.

He and his like would have had offices in London and shipped wool in bales to their stores in Calais, which was still English territory. In the church there are three brasses which depict sheep and wool packs at various of the benefactors' feet. The earlier Fortey brass is mid-fifteenth century. The setting of the town in a fold of the hills is unsurpassed, and the top of its great tower can be seen from miles around.

The town of Stow-on-the-Wold has a rather different history. It was founded as a commercial enterprise by the Abbey of Evesham in the middle of the eleventh century. The market received its royal grant in 1107. It was a major road junction, and the wide market square suggests a considerable attempt to exploit the commercial possibilities in the middle of the wool-producing Cotswolds. By the late fifteenth century there were two annual fairs. Its later growth followed from the relative prosperity of agriculture in general, the success of the local boot and shoe trade, and the wealth derived from its many inns. Stow is now

STANWAY House

to a considerable extent a dormitory town, its inhabitants going daily to work elsewhere and in the summer it is a centre for tourists. The layout remains medieval with narrow streets entering the market-place inconspicuously at the corners. The splendid church has work of all periods and a Perpendicular tower. A somewhat similar but far more interesting town architecturally is Tetbury. There are many fine houses in Long Street with gabled Tudor, Jacobean and Georgian fronts, leading up to a small market house on to which other streets converge. The wool market was important, so close is it to the Stroud valleys. Of modern development there is practically nothing except a new housing estate.

The Cotswolds are well known for possessing a large number of small manor-houses. The romantic grey gabled manor house and its yew trees is a nostalgic symbol for anyone who has known and loved this part of the world and been separated from it. The image has been fostered by some novels of John Buchan, and in the last war, by Robert Henriques. F. L. Griggs's drawing of Owlpen Manor and its great yews is the epitome of romance. The nearer the Cotswold edge the more romantic and west-country they seem. Owlpen is in a remote and beautiful valley not far from the Severn. Ernest Gimson and the Barnsley brothers were lured from London at the beginning of the century, and moved to Pinbury Park, which has perhaps the most perfect setting of any Cotswold house, above the hanging beech woods of Sapperton, described by Alfred Powell as a "mystery land of difficult hills and deeply wooded valleys dividing the vale of the White Horse from the Severn and the Welsh borderland". Here, assisted by Peter Waals, and other craftsmen, they produced beautifully finished furniture. A near-contemporary, Detmar Blow, was moved to build himself a house on the very edge of the escarpment in the traditional style but with an extra touch of genius all his own. On the other side of Painswick Beacon stands Prinknash Abbey described by Horace Walpole in 1774 with words still applicable today. "It stands on a glorious but impracticable hill, in the midst of a little forest of beech, and commanding Elysium." Many of the best houses are in fact on the escarpment edge preferably at the bottom, like Stanway with its superb gatehouse of golden ashlar decorated with carved scallop shells and Stanton Court set in one of the most perfectly preserved villages of all.

Many of the Cotswold villages, like the Slaughters and Bourton-on-the-Water, are well known for their picturesque qualities. Pope spoke of the pleasant prospect of Bibury; but it was William Morris who "discovered" it, and thought it the most beautiful village in England. The process was continued by Arthur Gibbs who published *A Cotswold Village* in 1898 when he lived at Ablington Manor. This was the first and best book to popularize the Cotswolds. Now "all connoisseurs put Bibury on their short list of villages that might be the most beautiful in England. Arlington Row and Swan Cottages are renowned among the reasons why this is so; but the bridge over the Coln, and Arlington Mill standing near it, are equally crucial to the composition". (Statement by the Ministry of Public Building and Works.) The cottages are mostly sixteenth and seventeenth century in origin and those in Arlington Row, which may be earlier, were occupied by weavers who supplied cloth for fulling at the Mill. Two mills are recorded at Arlington in the Domesday survey, which means two pairs of mill-stones (under one roof). The mill has a very long leat, probably constructed by the monks of Osney. It was always a corn-mill, and only combined fulling as well for a short time in the seventeenth and early eighteenth centuries. In the nineteenth century it was the largest and busiest corn-mill in the district so that power had to be augmented by a steam engine. It is now a country museum, and the water meadows are a flourishing trout farm.

In the eighteenth century Gloucestershire produced none of those great Whig families who built palaces on their coalfields. The very large houses in the county were built either at the beginning or the end of the century. Badminton was already of considerable size when Kent

DYRHAM Park

added its final embellishments. Dyrham was built by William III's Secretary of State, Blathwayt, and finished in 1704 by the fashionable architect Talman. The third great house, Dodington, was not finished till *c.* 1812. As for the owners of these estates, one was an almost royal duke, one a political upstart from the Netherlands, and Codrington of Dodington had made a fortune in the West Indies. Of the slightly smaller mansions, Barnsley, Barrington, Northwick and Sandywell are perhaps the most notable. Barnsley was built between 1720 and 1731 by Henry Perrot, a friend of the first Duke of Chandos and married to his niece. There is therefore a strong link with the Duke's great house Cannons, building at the same time, which probably explains the high quality of the Baroque architecture both inside and out. Barrington was built in 1738 for Earl Talbot with the money of his wife Mary de Cardonell, whose father had a post in the Government. They presumably employed Kent, though conclusive documentary evidence is still lacking. Northwick had reached substantial proportions by 1686, before it was partly remodelled by Lord Burlington for Sir John Rushout, in 1730, and altered *c.* 1778 by John Woolfe who designed the south bow windows and the domed staircase. Sandywell, like Barnsley, was finished before Burlington's Palladian influence swept all before it. It has wings built in the manner of Gibbs by some master-builder for Lord Conway, ancestor of the Earls of Hertford. Two splendid houses were built at the end of the century by S. P. Cockerell, Daylesford, and Sezincote, which is actually early nineteenth century and probably the most famous of all. Daylesford was the home of Warren Hastings and begun in 1787, but not in the Indian style; perhaps his trial was proving so painful he did not wish it. Sezincote was built for the architect's brother Sir Charles Cockerell who had made a fortune in the service of the East India Company and set up as a country gentleman. They had the help of Thomas Daniell, the Indian topographical artist, and Humphry Repton who had produced Indian designs for the remodelling of the Brighton Pavilion. It can be seen therefore that Gloucester-

shire's stately homes are in no way connected with the wealth of the former wool merchants whose families had died out, or gone into obscurity. Some elegant houses however were built by successful clothiers in the eighteenth century, particularly in the Stroud-Painswick district. For instance Pitchcombe House was built in 1740 and the grander Brownshill Court, *c.* 1777, by the same clothier family as they grew richer.

To complete this short survey of the county's architecture, mention must now be made of several nineteenth-century mansions, and churches. All the top Victorian architects did something in the county; but the two London (or anyway not local) architects who seem to have had most Gloucestershire clients were S. S. Teulon and Henry Woodyer, both extremely interesting and eccentric personalities. Teulon was a Londoner of French descent, born in 1812. The Ecclesiologists in general approved of him. He seems to have been a devout family man who was only wild in his working drawings, and very wild he could be. He attempted to create new forms out of medieval precedent, and many of his churches have Gothic tracery never seen before or since. It is this quality which makes him so attractive today and not his more orthodox designs. Huntley church is a fine example of the former, and Woodchester of the latter. His largest house was for Lord Ducie at Tortworth, and it appears far more significant and interesting than many other large houses designed at this time, 1849–52. It must have been congenial for Teulon to have such a go-ahead and ascetic client, as neither of them felt bound by the dictates of good taste, in common parlance, at Tortworth, they "had a ball". In spite of all its exuberance, however, the house betrays a characteristic Victorian seriousness.

Henry Woodyer was born in 1816, educated at Eton and Oxford, and became one of Butterfield's only two pupils. He was a distinguished-looking man, tall, rather spare, always attired in an easy-fitting blue serge suit, loose shirt collar, and crimson silk tie. His soft black hat, rather wide in the brim, bore a small steel brooch in front. During inclement weather a long dark Inverness cloak was worn. A most picturesque bearded figure often smoking an extremely fragrant cigar, he lived the life of a country gentleman in Surrey and had an intense dislike of anything which savoured of professionalism. In later life he would not have wished to cross Butterfield's doorstep. This was the architect the cultured Thomas Gambier-Parry employed to design his church at Highnam in 1849, and whose combined achievement—for Gambier-Parry painted the internal polychromy—has been described by Goodhart-Rendel as the fulfilment of the Pugin ideal. Gambier-Parry used to tell a story of how one day when he was painting the chancel walls dressed in an overall, two visitors approached and remarked, "Now we can see Mr Gambier-Parry does not do the painting himself." He had in fact made a study of the technique used by Italian painters of the fourteenth and fifteenth centuries, and invented "spirit fresco", suitable for wall painting in the English climate. His hopes have proved well founded, and the frescoes have retained their freshness to a remarkable degree; better perhaps than some of G. F. Bodley's interior decorations, though Bodley's churches in Gloucestershire at France Lynch and Selsley and the south aisle at Bussage are very early works, and before he started on his great schemes for wall painting in his later churches. Woodyer also built the vicarage, school, and a delightful lodge at Highnam, all showing his rare individuality. The school at Upton St Leonards is also characteristic, nor can one help admiring Minsterworth church, completely rebuilt by him in 1870, though in a very simple country style compared with the elaborations at Highnam.

G. E. Street's magnificent church at Toddington, golden ashlar outside, white inside, stands in the park of the earlier mansion designed by the amateur architect Charles Hanbury-Tracy, Lord Sudeley of Toddington. The house is picturesque Gothic but rather scholarly; he was influenced by the Oxford colleges in his youth and the publications of the elder Pugin. Hatherop Castle was rebuilt by Henry Clutton; not so good as the

church where he was helped by Burges. Vulliamy's Westonbirt is an enormous Victorian Elizabethan house used extensively to entertain Royalty at Edwardian shooting parties, and now a famous girls' school which still maintains the Victorian gardens as they used to be.

Of the local Victorian architects Benjamin Bucknall, who designed Woodchester Park, is the most interesting. He is known as the translator into English of the writings of Viollet-le-Duc; but of his architectural practice little has been discovered till recently. He was born at Rodborough in 1833, and was employed as a very young man to build the mansion in Woodchester Park, originally planned by Pugin, for the Roman Catholic William Leigh. The house stands in a remote and wooded valley near Nailsworth and has never been inhabited, as Leigh ran out of money before it was finished. It is built of the most superb stone probably, from Minchinhampton, and true to the precepts of Viollet-le-Duc all the construction is apparent. The completed rooms are stone-vaulted and others were intended to be, and the mullioned and transomed windows have splendid Gothic rere arches. Everything is made of stone including the rain-water gutters and down-pipes, and even the bath. The monastic buildings at Woodchester, again originally planned by Pugin, were finished by Charles Hansom. Other local buildings by Bucknall include several cottages on the Woodchester–Nympsfield estate, Tocknells House near Painswick, and St Rose's Convent, Stroud. He later retired to Algiers where there is still a street named after him, and built many villas for French and Arab clients. The most prolific church architect was John Middleton, of Cheltenham, where he designed no less than five new churches, besides building others in the county, such as the beautiful church at Clearwell for the Countess of Dunraven, and altering many others. The Medland-Maberley firm did a lot of ecclesiastical work; but Medland's best achievements are classical, such as the entrance to the Eastgate market in Gloucester and the front of the Corn Hall in Cirencester. The Waller family of Gloucester was a powerful architectural dynasty in ecclesiastical circles, particularly as they were architects in charge of the Cathedral. The middle Waller was married to a daughter of Professor Huxley. They cannot however be considered aesthetically reliable restorers as they were inclined to scrape the plaster off the interior walls of medieval churches. The Society for the Protection of Ancient Buildings, or Anti-Scrape Society, was founded by William Morris and his friends in protest against the proposed scraping of Tewkesbury Abbey, though this was by Sir Gilbert Scott.

At the end of the century the Cotswold manor-house style was ripe for revival. Webb's Red House for Morris was already many decades old. Webb apparently did nothing in Gloucestershire himself except for the alterations at Forthampton Court, and of course the windows for Bodley at Selsley; but he was a friend of Gimson and the Barnsleys, whose work and influence, carried on by Norman Jewson, went on up till the Second World War. Another revival was started by Sir Ernest George at Batsford for Lord Redesdale. Here the young Guy Dawber was employed as clerk of works, and here he learned all the local techniques for building in stone, and was later to build many houses himself in the neighbourhood. Copiers are legion; in fact it is hardly considered decent to build in any other style in the Cotswolds, even though the material is no longer natural. The charge of "preciousness" is not without foundation in some places, and in Chipping Campden—largely as a result of Ashbee's Guild of Handicraft and Griggs's Campden Trust—it is not always easy to determine what is old and what is new. However, at the other extreme, for example in Stroud, the recent casualty list of old houses has been enormous.

Of the more curious buildings the canal systems provide their quota. The long disused Thames-Severn Canal runs across the Cotswolds from Lechlade to Sapperton, where it enters the tunnel in a wood a hundred yards off the Coates–Tarlton road. Doric columns with niches, roundels and a rusticated archway mark the entrance, with an exit at Sapperton in simple Gothic style. It was first used in 1789. The journey from Lechlade is punctuated by round tower-like buildings used as maintenance men's houses, and at Kempsford and Cirencester there are wharfs, with wharfingers' houses. The canal was not used after 1911. A series of locks took the canal down to the Stroudwater Canal, passing Brimscombe where Robert Whitworth provided a warehouse and offices only recently demolished. The Stroudwater Canal ended at Framilode on the Severn (where there is a typical row of boatmen's cottages) after crossing the Gloucester–Berkeley canal designed by Telford and Mylne, who were responsible for the many little neo-Greek canal houses which look like Doric temples.

This was the age of follies, and Gloucestershire possesses one of the most spectacular triumphs of all park buildings in the Worcester Lodge at Badminton. Here Kent provided a superb Palladian room over the archway, intended as a summer dining room. Many of the barns on the estate look like miniature castles with their battlemented parapets. Ragged Castle, however, is nothing but a folly, perhaps by Thomas Wright, c. 1750. Cirencester Park also is full of follies, and has the earliest of all in Alfred's Hall, built in 1721. It is true sham and Lord Bathurst delighted in "the real horrid feeling of conglomeration". Obelisks there were too, one right in the town, only a few yards from Cotswold Avenue. Another also of 1721, is in a wood at Nether Lypiatt, near Bisley, commemorating the death of a horse.

Like most counties Gloucestershire is rich in church monuments. The fourteenth century produced a magnificent series of monuments in Tewkesbury Abbey, second only to those at Westminster. The three chantry chapels are the culmination of the group which includes the recumbent effigies of Hugh Despencer who died in 1348 and his wife, under a canopy comparable to that of Edward II in Gloucester Cathedral. The King's effigy is London work of c. 1330. There are also very fine effigies at Coberley and Leckhampton of Knights and their ladies of this

The east entrance to the tunnel on the Thames and Severn canal, COATES

period. Berkeley has effigies of the Lords of Berkeley, and at Wotton-under-Edge are some very good Berkeley brasses of *c.* 1392. Other fourteenth-century effigies are to be found at Minchinhampton, Longborough, Whittington, Newland, Pucklechurch, Shipton Moyne, Winterbourne, and at Old Sodbury there is a wooden effigy of a knight. Usually the nearer to Bristol the more skilful the sculptor. The wooden effigy of Robert Duke of Normandy in the cathedral is rather earlier. Perhaps the most interesting monuments of the fifteenth century are the brasses, and these mostly belong to the wool merchants at Chipping Campden, Cirencester, Northleach and Lechlade. The earliest brass is that of a Lady at Winterbourne, *c.* 1370. Other brasses are at Deerhurst, Dyrham, Newland, Rodmarton, Sevenhampton, Tornarton, and Blockley where there is a rare figure of a priest of 1510 in full mass vestments. Brasses continued to be made in the sixteenth century; there are examples at Berkeley, Bisley, Cold Ashton, St Mary's Cheltenham, Dowdeswell, Eastington, Mitcheldean, Minchinhampton, Newent, Northleach and Olveston, and after the Reformation, a Philip and Mary brass at Whittington. A couple of late brasses worth mentioning are one at Yate, *c.* 1590, and a lady in a four-poster bed, 1605, at Wormington. There are not many early indications of the coming of the Renaissance in church monuments, such was the cultural separation of England from Europe due to Henry VIII's policies. However, the tomb of Thomas Throckmorton, who died in 1568, at Tortworth, shows the classical style overtaking the Gothic, and the Lygon monument at Fairford is decorated with strapwork, *c.* 1560. At Sapperton there is a monument by Guildo of Hereford with a Renaissance canopy dated 1574. Such others are the tombs of Edward Veele at Almonsbury, George Wynter at Dyrham, the Lloyds at Ampney Crucis, the Stratfords at Farmcote and the Tryes at Hardwicke.

The beginning of the seventeenth century was a period of prosperity. Samuel Baldwin of Stroud was a successful imitator of the Southwark workshops. His monuments in the cathedral include two married daughters of the Bishop, in the Lady Chapel. He also has works at Avening (Henry Brydges who died in 1615), at Berkeley, the Kingston monument at Miserden, another at St Laurence's, Stroud, at Painswick, and in the Lady Chapel at Cirencester. At St Nicholas, Gloucester, there are the effigies of Alderman Wallton and his wife, she in a tall hat like Mrs Bridges at Cirencester. Grander monuments in the manner of Nicholas Stone are those of the de la Beres at Bishop's Cleeve, the Campdens at Chipping Campden, Alderman Blackleech in the cathedral, and the Sandys monument at Miserden. At Sapperton there is a splendid canopied monument like a Renaissance four-poster bed with many effigies and much heraldry to Sir Henry Poole and his family, probably London work of *c.* 1616. The shrouded figures of the first Viscount Campden and his wife at Chipping Campden is signed by Joshua Marshall, 1664. At Cirencester there is the reclining effigy of Sir Thomas Master, died 1680, a life-size figure in deshabillé and a wig, and at Sapperton the county historian Sir Robert Atkyns who died in 1711. The grandest of all is the Grinling Gibbons monument at Badminton to the first Duke of Beaufort, moved from Windsor.

Churchyard memorials of this time are some of the best in England. Painswick is deservedly the most well known, with table tombs of all shapes and sizes, some even resembling the silver tea-caddies of the period. The Painswick masons provided tombstones even further afield. Elmore in the Gloucester Vale, has most notable examples with sculpture of great accomplishment and imagination, carved in Painswick stone. Cotswold oolitic limestone carves very deep, but sometimes has poor resistance to weather, and it is quite usual to find engraved lettering on small brass plaques attached to the stone. These brasses are often of considerable merit and have qualities derived from intaglio prints. One, as far away as Barnsley, is signed by a Painswick artist. They make good use of the medium in evolving complex and highly decorative letter forms. There are good examples at Miserden, King's Stanley and many other places.

Edward II, GLOUCESTER Cathedral

Great Georgian monuments inside the churches are probably not so numerous as in other counties, but those there are have much interest. At Great Badminton there are the life-size statues of the Dukes of Beaufort in Roman togas, by Rysbrack. At Blockley we find busts by Rysbrack to the owners of Northwick Park, and at Sherborne Rysbrack made a full-length figure of Sir John Dutton. Nollekens was commissioned to make busts of Countess Talbot at Great Barrington, and of the Earl and Countess Bathurst at Cirencester. The splendid monument at Upton St Leonards to Sir Thomas Snell is by the talented

Gloucester firm of Ricketts, who did many works in the neighbourhood. Of the lesser local sculptors Pearce of Frampton-on-Severn produced many charming tablets with weeping willows and other symbols of death and resurrection. Large numbers of beautiful tablets were made by the Bristol family of Paty, and there are many examples of work by Thomas King of Bath. Nineteenth-century monuments include the bust of Sir Onesiphorus Paul and the statue of Jenner both by Sievier, in the cathedral, the recumbent effigy of Queen Katharine Parr by J. Birnie Philip at Sudeley and that of Lady de

37

Mauley by Raffaelle Monti at Hatherop. Henry Wilson, the architect, is well represented in the cathedral in the monument to Canon Tinling who died in 1897.

Gloucestershire campanology is interesting. From the thirteenth century the bell-foundries in Bristol and Gloucester were the most important in England, and the great majority of the bells in local towers are from one or the other. Abraham Rudhall of Gloucester was in his day just about the best English bell-founder. His career extended over fifty years (1684–1735), during which time he probably cast more large rings and a higher gross total of bells than any single founder on record. The Rudhalls sold to Thomas Mears of London in 1830.

People come from all over the world to see the stained glass at Fairford, now only a mile or so from the Concorde's runway. Every window is filled with its original glass made for it by the school of Henry VII's Master Glass Painster, Barnard Flower. The entire history of the Christian faith is told in consecutive order round the church, with exquisitely coloured figures before the entrancing backgrounds of Flemish cities mixed with English Perpendicular architecture. At Rendcomb the glass, though fragmentary, is interesting for being a little later than Fairford, and showing Renaissance details. There is no very early glass in the county unless some fragments at Sudeley are thirteenth century, and the earliest seems to be at Arlingham where saints on plain ruby grounds under canopies with borders date from the beginning of the fourteenth century, and are similar to the little St Catherine window at Deerhurst. The most complete and beautiful glass of this period is in the clerestory windows of the presbytery at Tewkesbury Abbey, with figures of knights intended to be portraits of the de Clare and Despencer families. The great east window in the cathedral contains the largest quantity of glass, c. 1350; it represents the Coronation of the Virgin and has row upon row of hierarchical figures standing under canopies totally devoid

of perspective, and below is the heraldry of the lords who fought at the Battle of Crecy. The glazier used white, blue, yellow and red glass. The white is full of bubbles giving that silvery light which is so apparent in this window. The blue was pure pot-metal, so that it is blue throughout. The ruby glass would have been nearly opaque if it had been red all through, so a different process was invented to produce flashed ruby glass. A yellow stain was also used which was lighter than the pot-metal and varied in many shades. For line shading a brown enamel, made from iron, was used, or copper if a greenish black was required. It is not so much the development of technique, however, which is remarkable in this window, as the development of design. The great Perpendicular window determined the design of the glass. It is the first and grandest example of a window filled with tiers of full-length figures. The subject and its treatment are somewhat the same as Orcagna's contemporary triptych in the National Gallery.

Most medieval glass to survive in the county is fifteenth century. The east window at Cirencester has glass from Siddington church of c. 1480. There is very beautiful glass of this period at Bledington, at Buckland, and at North Cerney; small quantities are also to be found at Bagendon, Coln Rogers, Dyrham, Frampton-on-Severn, Iron Acton, Stanton, Hailes, Temple Guiting and Tortworth; besides fragments in many other places, including Sudeley Castle where the nineteenth-century owners collected. There is some sixteenth-century glass in one of the windows in the cloister of Gloucester Cathedral. Woodforde writes: "A much higher standard was maintained in the sixteenth century in drawing of heraldry than figures." Here are excellent examples, some Royal, like the pomegranate badge of Katharine of Aragon, and some to do with the family of Brydges, Lords Chandos of Sudeley. These panels came from Prinknash Abbey, where the chapel retains a sixteenth-century window of the Nine Choirs of Angels. Most of the windows in the cloisters are by Hardman, which brings us to the nineteenth century.

Poole monument, SAPPERTON

39

The Victorian glass in the cathedral is very conspicuous. The huge west window with its strident colours is by Wailes of Newcastle, completed in 1859. In the nave are good examples of Hardman and Clayton & Bell; the more unpalatable are by Bell of Bristol, and Warrington. In St Paul's Chapel are three windows by Burlison & Grylls, 1870. In the ambulatory the windows are by Kempe. The Lady Chapel has fine glass by Christopher Whall, with an east window composed of fragments of the fourteenth and fifteenth centuries. Victorian glass is to be found in most churches. Particularly excellent are the windows by William Morris & Co at Selsley, by Clayton & Bell at Daylesford, George Rogers of Worcester at Fretherne, and the marvellous east window in St Mary de Crypt, Gloucester, by Rogers imitating the medieval, Willement's heraldic windows at Great Badminton, more Willement at Haresfield, Thornbury, and Barnsley where it alternates with Wailes, a rose-window in Cheltenham parish church by Wailes, Burlison & Grylls' east window at Dursley, Hardman at Cirencester David Evans at Upton St Leonards, some by Heaton, Butler & Bayne like the east window at Charfield, Kempe at Bourton-on-the-Water, and many other places, Powell at Tortworth, and coming into the present century, Comper at Eastington, Stanton, Whaddon and Rangeworthy, Bewsey at St Laurence, Stroud, F. C. Eden at North Cerney, Henry Payne at Chipping Campden and Turkdean, H. J. Stammers at Sandhurst, and Geoffrey Webb at Shipton Sollars. It is difficult to explain how to distinguish Victorian glass artists one from another, particularly in certain cases between Hardman and Clayton & Bell, and Powell windows also present problems, as these firms worked over such a long period and employed so many different artists. Usually the earlier ones are the best. One can only learn by looking.

Gloucestershire has its quota of Nonconformist chapels; but being a district generally rich in architecture the remark that "chapels make an unmemorable village stay in the mind" is not so applicable as elsewhere. Memorable chapels there are, however, particularly in the cloth towns near Stroud, such as those at Chalford, King's Stanley, Nailsworth, Painswick, Rodborough, Uley and Stroud itself, more near Bristol, at Frenchay, Kingswood and Hanham, and the Victorian ones in Cheltenham.

Gardens and Arboreta

It was a famous remark of either Elwes or Henry that most of the finest collections of trees in Britain were within 20 miles of Gloucester or Perth. Actually their own records show that Ware or Hertford and Exeter were even better centres; but it remains true that Gloucestershire is very well provided with arboreta.

Firstly, and most important, there is the supreme collection in Britain—Westonbirt. For more than fifty years (1839–92) Robert Staynor Holford owned the Westonbirt estate, and in that time he completely transformed the landscape. He began planting the one hundred and fourteen acres of arboretum before 1839. In 1840–50 he laid out new gardens, and was obliged to move the village to a different site as it got in the way of his plans for terraces and formal borders. This Victorian garden survives and is well looked after by Westonbirt School. The village was rebuilt by Holford's London architect Lewis Vulliamy. The garden contains many fine specimen trees including the oldest Japanese Horse Chestnut (*Aesculus turbinata*) in Britain. The most spectacular times to visit the arboretum are spring and autumn. For the best trees see the list in the Appendix.

Next after Westonbirt is the rival estate of Tortworth planted by Holford's friend the second Earl of Ducie who had sold his estate Woodchester Park in 1845, and employed S. S. Teulon to build a new house at Tortworth, 1849–52. Lord Ducie was extremely go-ahead. He was an advanced Liberal Member of Parliament before he succeeded to the title. Rich and happily married he was master of foxhounds, hunting his own hounds with great zeal, exceedingly passionate and injudicious in his language, and a scientific and practical farmer.

The progeny of his shorthorn herd have lasted till the present day. He started an "example" farm to "open the eyes of farmers to the value of improvements". He opened works at Uley for the manufacture of agricultural implements, one of which, the Ducie Cultivator, was his own invention, and he either invented or developed the lawn-mower. He ended up "very religious" and died aged only 51. This was the man who planted the Tortworth arboretum, which was altogether better than Holford's at the time, and which even now surpasses Westonbirt for oak species and a few others.

There is a small but good pine collection at Highnam, near Gloucester, which belonged to the Gambier-Parry family, better known in the world of art and music than arboriculture. Thomas Gambier-Parry started his Pinetum in 1844, when little was known about Coniferae, and most specimens had to be grown from seed. By 1853 he was able to list 385 specimens. The site sloped to the south, and though in part clay, was in one direction light and sandy. The gardens were laid out by James Pulham, who used a Portland stone cement of his own, which he called Pulhamite, before 1850, and an extensive rock garden of this material still exists.

The splendid arboretum at Batsford Park was made in the nineteenth century by Lord Redesdale, and the gardens have ornamental Buddhas and a Chinese temple. The house was designed by Sir Ernest George, 1888–92, with Guy Dawber as clerk of works, and is an early example—if not the first—of the "Cotswold style".

Other country houses have a few big trees, such as Stanway, Huntley Manor, and Williamstrip Park; there is a good small collection at Speech House and there are occasional notable roadside trees and oddments like the Newland oak. Besides these there are the two great eighteenth-century parks at Cirencester and Badminton. At Cirencester the entrance front of the mansion is only separated from the street by an enormous semi-circle of yew hedge, a conceit typical of the first Lord Bathurst, whose interests were more horticultural than architectural. He developed the park in collaboration with Pope and other friends who it is said furnished him with "most convincing arguments drawn from classical precedent". His own first-hand experience of the growth of trees supplied the necessary practical knowledge. It is the finest surviving example in England of planting in the "pre-landscape" manner and was started just when geometrical avenues were beginning to be thought old-fashioned and continued till 1775 when Capability Brown's system of naturalism itself was being called in question.

A list of specimen trees in the county (excluding Cirencester Park), selected for their outstanding size or rarity, by Alan F. Mitchell, appears in the Appendix on p. 130.

The most historical garden is the formal Dutch garden at Westbury-on-Severn, which has just been rescued from total disappearance by the National Trust. It has a straight canal with a pavilion at one end rebuilt by Robert Paterson and a parallel canal with a T-shaped end where there are clairvoyees flanked by pillars with pineapple finials.

At Hidcote the National Trust owns the most trend-setting garden of the century. It is the creation of Lawrence Johnston who began in about 1905. V. Sackville-West described it as resembling "a series of cottage gardens in so far as the plants grow in a jumble, flowering shrubs mingled with roses, herbaceous plants with bulbous subjects, climbers scrambling over hedges, a kind of haphazard luxuriance, which of course comes neither by hap or hazard at all". Most people have now turned towards flowering shrubs and trees, and roses-grown-as-shrubs; but Lawrence Johnston was one of the first.

Gazetteer

The number after each entry refers to the square on the map where the place is to be found

Abenhall (2). Medieval sandstone church on the edge of the Forest of Dean. Pretty approach from Flaxley, not so good from Mitcheldean past a modern County Secondary School. Still crisp headstones in the churchyard. Fifteenth-century octagonal font with pairs of vertical quatrefoils in lozenges, and shields on the chamfers with incised devices of the freeminers. Brasses of early seventeenth-century date, Richard Pyrke and his wife and two sons; also early eighteenth-century Baroque tablet to later Pyrkes, with small Ionic columns standing on piled books. Jumbled fragments of good quality mid-fourteenth-century glass, probably St Catherine. Another north window by Bryans. One mile south-south-east of Mitcheldean.

Ablington (14). Manor house in heavenly situation on the river Coln. The gabled porch has inscription "Plead Thou my cause, Oh Lord, by John Coxwel Ano Domeny 1590", above a Renaissance doorway with heads in the frieze, including Elizabeth I's. Rendered, and coloured in traditional yellow ochre. Occupied by Arthur Gibbs, author of *A Cotswold Village*, before First World War. Magnificent barns. North of the village a long barrow and beehive chamber. One mile north-west of Bibury.

Abson (8). Pretty Perpendicular tower with battlements, pinnacles and image-niches; six bells, two of them of pre-Reformation date. Otherwise mixed Norman, Early English and Tudor. Sculptures—anthropophagous on the south face of the tower, something else on the east wall of the chancel.

Acton Turville (9). Very near Badminton. Inescapable signs of the Establishment. Church much restored by the Salisbury diocesan architect T. H. Wyatt, in 1853; but a most remarkable Early English bell-cote survives, with spirelet and pinnacles.

Adlestrop (15). Railway station opened in 1853; on a main line but trains do not stop. Express trains never did, hence the line in Edward Thomas's poem when his train did stop "unwontedly" at Adlestrop. A big house rebuilt by Sanderson Miller in 1762, in symmetrical early Gothic-revival style. Grounds laid out by Humphry Repton. Cedars and elms. Jane Austen visited her uncle Theophilus Leigh at the rectory. Church has had frequent rebuildings including one by Sanderson Miller. Leigh family hatchments and tablets.

Alderley (16). Long the property of the Hale family descended from a Lord Chief Justice of 1671. Two good Georgian houses in the village. The Grange built in 1744, with wings added *c.* 1810, and a rear portion dated 1608. The Mount of two different building dates in the eighteenth century. Both with established and well-loved gardens, the latter made by Marianne North, the botanical artist and collector. There is a sundial monument to her opossum mouse. The church was rebuilt in 1802 (except for the Perpendicular tower) with a broad auditorium, ribbed plaster ceiling with gold-leaf bosses and corbels, apsidal sanctuary, Gothic windows with original glass in the intersecting tracery, and a castellated parapet outside. Group of monumental tablets, including a draped Neo-Greek one by Sir Francis Chantry, and the latest by Bryant Fedden is a worthy addition. The churchyard has five fine table-tombs, three very early and one made of marble in the eighteenth century. Pretty pink marble headstone to Marianne North, 1890. Rosehill School, next the church, was built in 1860 by Lewis Vulliamy. A pretty road descends on the village from Tresham. Good views over the Berkeley Vale.

Alderton (11). Country Tewkesbury-Evesham Vale and Cotswold outliers.

Traditional building in both stone and half-timber, new housing in reconstructed stone. Church over-restored in 1890 by Knight and Chatters of Cheltenham. Dixton Manor, 2 miles south-west, is only about half its original size, ending in what was a central tall gabled stone porch, which retains its date-inscription of 1555.

Aldsworth (15). A particularly interesting little church, the most notable feature being the late Perpendicular north aisle added by the Abbey of Osney, on to a Norman arcade. This was a chapel and there is an excellently preserved niche which once held the image of St Catherine (her wheel is carved on the pedestal). On the east wall of the porch is another niche but of a different kind, and in a position common to this district and late Perpendicular date. It has a pierced stone cresset to hold candles and may be a poor man's chantry. Three pre-Reformation bells, thought to be early fifteenth century and by Robert Hendly of Gloucester, and also a Sanctus bell on the east side of the spire. The village seen from the main road has a distinctly early nineteenth-century look and this is because the most prominent houses were built during the hey-day of the Bibury Race-course on the opposite bank, when considerable accommodation for grooms and jockeys must have been required. The last flock of pedigree Cotswold sheep survive here.

Almondsbury (8). Now famous for the Almondsbury Interchange which is the first four-level motorway crossing in Britain, opened by the Queen in 1966. On the Almondsbury-Tormarton section of the M4 twenty-four bridges were built by 1966, and two viaducts over the river Frome at Hambrook of similar design in reinforced concrete. Bridges carry

Barns: ASHLEWORTH and ABLINGTON

42

county roads over the motorways in a single span. They are of composite design having pre-stressed concrete abutments which cantilever out over the motorway to carry a suspended span formed of pre-cast pre-stressed concrete beams. The church is set under the side of the hill and has a tall lead broach spire. The Early English chancel has been much restored. C. E. Ponting designed the carved reredos in 1891. He was also the architect for the Cottage Hospital in the manner of Norman Shaw. Knole Park still has a romantic outline against the sky with its fifteenth-century tower overlooking the Severn, but close-to it is depressing, with speculatively-built small "rustic" houses coming right up to the front door. Over Court, too, has deteriorated; there is a detached tumbledown archway of mid-eighteenth-century date, with a pediment surmounted by an obelisk standing on a scrolled plinth. The manor house at Gaunt's Earthcott serves delicious dinners. A house called "The Portico" at Patchway was moved from Frenchay, a most unhappy change of location as it has turned out, for the parish is effectively cut up by the motorways.

Alstone (11). Norman church restored in 1880 with Perpendicular north arcade, Early English east end, and porch dated 1621, which may also be the date of most of the windows; the interior walls are scraped. The village has pretty timber-framed houses with orchards, at the foot of Woolstone Hill, and is approached by what is still not much more than a winding lane, in rather uninteresting country.

Alveston (8). Identity almost lost to the A38 carrying M5 traffic; however, it is worth pulling in to the Ship Hotel which is now a thriving motel and restaurant. The old church has been demolished except for the tower, but some of its furnishings have gone into the 1885 rock-faced church, situated so close to the road that only the most determined would dare stop.

Alvington (5). Sliced in half by the A48. The church is set back and has Early English and Decorated features,

though over-restored, and now looks Victorian. The south aisle is as broad as the nave.

Amberley (16). On the edge of Minchinhampton Common, with views over the Woodchester valley. Hanson's monastic buildings look best from here. The church is of 1836, and served a scattered residential area of long standing. Bracing air, hotels, golf and riding.

Ampney Crucis (17). Till recently very much part of an estate, now most of the houses are owned by their occupiers. The church has features of all periods including Saxon, and contains a Jacobean monument with effigies. There is a well-known cross in the churchyard with more or less intact imagery which escaped the Puritans by being carefully walled-up inside the church till it was discovered by a Tractarian clergyman. A corn-mill with machinery *in situ* survives on the Ampney Brook near the church. The parish is extensive and includes old sheep runs higher up on the Cotswolds, though the gradual decline here to the upper Thames is almost imperceptible.

Ampney St Mary (17). Isolated little church on the A417; inevitably rouses curiosity as there is no visible village, and there are several unusual features such as the strange primitive tympanum, the stone chancel screen with the elbow of a returned stall, the faded wall-painting intended to teach that work on Sunday is hurting to Christ, the flowing Decorated windows, and the stained glass by F. C. Eden, put in after a sympathetic restoration in 1913, since the church had fallen into complete disuse in Victorian times.

Ampney St Peter (17). Church has a Saxon nave and tower arch, chancel arch Norman; restored and north aisle added by Sir G. G. Scott in 1878. The village is compact and has some well-restored Cotswold houses.

Apperley (10). Romanesque style church of 1856 by F. C. Penrose, in brick with pink terracotta dressings; enlarged by him later on, and spoiled. Flat river-side country with orchards.

Arlingham (5). Situated in a loop of the Severn on the Gloucester side, a remote peninsula with the river taking nine miles to progress one. The church is interesting for its medieval glass, chandeliers and monuments. The glass dates from *c.* 1300, delicious reds and greens, and there is another lot of the C 15. The chandeliers are a magnificent pair made in Bristol *c.* 1770. The monuments include a sculptured mourning female by Nollekens in memory of Mary Yate who died in 1777. There are also particularly well-preserved churchyard headstones and table tombs, full of Baroque invention. The Yate family's house has disappeared, but one and a half miles west of the church there is a farmhouse called Wick Court which is quite large, half-timbered and brick, and has sixteenth- and seventeenth-century features.

Ashchurch (10). Church contains a rood-screen; since Bishop Hooper a comparatively rare feature in Gloucestershire churches. Fiddington Manor is timber-framed and was the house of William Ferrers whose monument in the church (he died in 1625) is London work. The Dovecote has gables with carved finials and a cupola. Yellow brick railway station with cast-iron "Gothic" details.

Ashleworth (13). Group of medieval buildings by the side of the Severn. The church has work of all periods, and a spire. The house is stone-built and dates from *c.* 1460. The tithe-barn a little later. It is practically unspoiled. Besides this there is another house in the village of 1460 which is half-timbered. There is a pub on the quay.

Ashley (16). Norman church, and seventeenth-century manor.

Aston Blank (14). High wold village. Norman church with blank east wall, Easter sepulchre, pretty Perpendicular tower, and Baroque monument.

Aston Magna (12). Shell of medieval church hidden in small house in village.

Aston-Subedge (5). Elm country at

the foot of the Cotswold scarp. Houses built in brick as well as stone. Church by Thomas Johnson of Warwick, 1797, but the windows altered later. Seventeenth-century manor where Endymion Porter entertained Prince Rupert for Dover's Games. Dover's Hill was where the Games took place from 1612 to 1852.

Aust (5). The Severn Bridge was opened by the Queen on September 8, 1966. It was designed by Sir Gilbert Roberts of Freeman Fox & Partners, in conjunction with Mott, Hay & Anderson. It is a revolutionary design in that the torsionally stiff box as described by the experts, combined with inclined suspenders provides aerodynamic stability, so that stiffening girders are not necessary. The resulting appearance is light and fragile. The accompanying road house is modern and good. Not much of a village left. The church is Perpendicular and has a fine tower.

Avening (6). Beautiful cruciform Norman church, with vaulted chancel. Monuments include the kneeling effigy of a notorious pirate by Baldwin of Stroud, and a collection of rustic Baroque tablets in the south transept, which is a kind of museum. A good Clayton & Bell east window and two nave windows by Christopher Whall. Avening Court has an Elizabethan-style façade no older than the end of the last century, but parts of the house are of greater antiquity and it is prettily situated in a combe.

Awre (5). A flat, thinly populated, extremely remote, farming district on the Dean bank of a loop of the Severn, with no villages. Church early thirteenth century with Perpendicular tower. Enormous "dug-out" chest used for laying-out bodies recovered from the river. Fieldhouse is a timber-framed farmhouse of partly cruck construction; most of the farms are probably seventeenth century. At Gatcombe a pretty riverside place, there is a house still called Sir Francis Drake's because it is said he came up the river (it must have been more navigable) to consult with Admiral Wynter at Lydney.

Aylburton (5). Fourteenth-century

church taken down and rebuilt retaining its ancient features in more convenient site in 1856.

Badgeworth (3). The north aisle has the best Decorated architecture of any parish church in the county, profusely ornamented with ball-flower. Bentham Manor has thirteenth-century archway probably not *in situ*.

Badminton House (9). *See* Great Badminton.

Bagendon (14). A little Norman church, with some Perpendicular alterations carried out by the Weavers' Company of Cirencester. Glass; some medieval bits, and a serene window by Whall, 1906. Trinity Mill, which is opposite the golf course, is on a Saxon site, with a long leat. Its machinery is *in situ*. Between it and the church was the capital of the Early Iron Age Dubunni, where they minted coins.

Barnsley (17). Specially pretty village only spoiled by heavy through traffic. No over-head wiring, but plenty of television. Norman church with upstanding Elizabethan tower; over-restored in Tractarian times. Organ by Samuel Green (1740–96). Fine mature trees and well-kept gardens. In Barnsley Park, an early Georgian Baroque mansion, which once housed Sir Isaac Newton's library, a conservatory and lodge designed by Nash, and the site of a long-established Roman villa with the undisturbed earthworks of a large Roman agricultural system. Barnsley House, in village, 1697, altered 1830.

Barnwood (13). Norman church with late Perpendicular tower, Decorated bellcote, and well-furnished interior with good Victorian glass by Clayton & Bell, Hardman, George Rogers of Worcester (his recurring theme of the four evangelists) and Veronica Whall. Victorian lunatic asylums demolished and their well-planted grounds developed for housing.

Barrington (15). Quarries of inferior oolite, extensively used in the past. Great Barrington church, Norman, quite spacious, late Perpendicular alterations, over-restored in 1880.

Monuments. Barrington Park landscaped and mansion probably designed by Kent. Little Barrington church Norman; sculptured north tympanum. Particularly attractive village set round a triangular green through which runs a stream. The two villages are divided by the Windrush and both have many examples of well-built stone cottages. The Grove is a Georgian estate in miniature.

Batsford (12). Mansion designed in the Cotswold idiom by George & Peto for Lord Redesdale, who made a fabulous garden. Stables also by Sir Ernest, horrifyingly eclectic. Neo-Romanesque church by chapel-builders from Reading complete with ditto wooden pew described by Goodhart-Rendel as the Holy Hons Cupboard.

Baunton (17). Small church notable for a quite well-preserved and restored St Christopher wall-painting, and also for the example of *Opus Anglicanum*, a complete and unaltered fifteenth-century frontal. The bellcote has two bells by Thomas Rudhall, 1776.

Beachley (4). Always was an exciting place at low tide and at the beginning of the flow when the upward current fights the Severn sluicing over the reef in its bed, now made all the more impressive by the great bridge flying overhead.

Berkeley (5). Castle begun in the eleventh century as a military building, but it is now mostly of the fourteenth century having been remodelled *c*. 1350. Edward II was murdered here in 1327. The great range of inhabitable apartments have been occupied ever since by the Berkeley family, albeit through almost continuous periods of domestic strife. Architecturally the most distinguished feature is the "Berkeley Arch". It is polygonal with four or more straight sides enclosing a cusped inner arch with usually slightly ogee-shaped foils. It is repeatedly used in doorways and windows. In the 'twenties the last Earl introduced a considerable amount of

Monument:
GREAT BARRINGTON

BERKELEY Castle

French medieval architecture in the form of windows, and even the main entrance doorway. The castle is open every day in the summer. The church has outstanding examples of thirteenth-century work, particularly the west end. There is a Perpendicular mortuary chapel with splendid monuments, and a detached eighteenth-century tower. The town is sleepy Georgian in spite of the activities caused by the building of the Atomic Power Station. Jenner's hut, where he first did vaccinations, is preserved in the vicarage garden.

Beverston (6). Remains of a thirteenth-century castle with some finely detailed architecture in the fourteenth-century chapel. The existing domestic wing was not built till after the Berkeleys left in 1597. The church's best feature is its south arcade which has early stiff-stalk capitals and its oldest object is the Saxon sculpture on the south face of the tower; but there are other intriguing features, not least Vulliamy's extraordinary roof trusses. The estate cottages in the village are also by Vulliamy.

Bibury (14). Pope spoke of the pleasant prospect of Bibury; but it was William Morris who "discovered" it, and thought it the most beautiful village in England. The process was continued by Arthur Gibbs, who published *A Cotswold Village* in 1898. All connoisseurs now put Bibury on their short list of villages that might be the most beautiful. Arlington Row (National Trust) and Swan Cottages are renowned among the reasons why this is so; but the bridge over the Coln, and Arlington Mill standing near it, are equally crucial to the composition. The Mill was recorded in Domesday; the existing building is seventeenth century, dating from when it was a cloth mill as well as a corn mill. It has a very long leat constructed when it belonged to Osney Abbey. The mill is now open to the public every day and has machinery in working order, besides a museum of arts and crafts, and Victoriana. Rack Isle, where the cloth was dried, is a bird sanctuary. Above is a trout farm, open to the public at week-ends in the summer. The Arlington Row cottages were occupied by weavers who supplied the cloth for fulling. The central cottages in the row are medieval with cruck trusses and stone spiral staircases. One has a carved stone Jacobean chimneypiece, another a large stone tank probably used for dyeing the cloth. Bibury is also one of the few places which still possesses considerable remains of its large Saxon church. Inside are the casts of two Saxon gravestones showing the Ringerike style of the early eleventh century; the originals are in the British Museum. The chancel arch has Saxon jambs and capitals. In the churchyard there are cedars, roses and table-tombs. Bibury Court (1633) is now an hotel.

Birdlip (13). At the top of a very steep descent down to the Gloucester vale, a point usually reached with relief by literary eighteenth-century travellers who welcomed the milder climate after crossing the windswept wolds. In fact, if it is sunny on the hills it can be foggy below, and vice versa. The beech trees are beautiful whatever the weather.

Bishops Cleeve (14). One of the largest and most splendid late-Norman or Transitional churches in the county. Turrets at the west end,

Arlington Mill, BIBURY

48

central tower rebuilt in 1700, and crossing with transepts. Long Decorated chancel. South porch has intersecting arcades, and a rich doorway with beasts' heads; above, an upper chamber has wall paintings done by a school-master in 1818, battle scenes with elephants. More wall paintings in the rectory, including a bride arriving in a carriage in 1810. The church also has an extremely fine Jacobean musicians' gallery, the best in the county—it is difficult to avoid superlatives. The rectory is the oldest parsonage house; it is thirteenth century in origin, built for the Bishop of Worcester, with a rectangular double dovecote, and half a tithe barn. A lot of new housing in the parish.

Bisley (6 & 13). Compact, hill-side stone-built village with several interesting houses. The church was over-restored in 1862 by Thomas Keble's curate, an amateur architect, whose explanation of the font was "the work of a carver whose happy ignorance of the art of modern stone carving has produced a spirited specimen of the rude Anglo-Norman of the nineteenth century". But there are other good things like the carved bosses in the vestry, the double Piscina, the Clayton & Bell glass, the brass of Katheryn Sewell, and the poor soul's light in the churchyard. Prettily situated below the churchyard are the well-heads with gushing spring water, and "traditions", invented, like the tale that Queen Elizabeth was a Bisley boy, by Mr Keble. It is a large parish with many outlying houses (built for successful clothiers) of which most have considerable architectural pretensions, like Over Court, Jaynes Court, Avenis Farm, Solomon's Court, Catswood, Ferris Court, Middle Lypiatt, Sydenhams, Lower Througham and Througham Slad. Nether Lypiatt Manor was built in 1702–5 and is the perfect "grand" house in miniature. Sacheverell Sitwell wrote: "No house would compose so beautifully for a glass transparency, with wrought iron gates in front flanked by a pair of little formal pavilions, and with an interior where music will forever linger for it was the home of Violet Gordon Woodhouse." Lypiatt Park dates from the fourteenth century with a detached chapel. It was enlarged by Wyatville and T. H. Wyatt. Waterlane House, built in the early nineteenth century by Thomas Baker, was enlarged by Ernest Gimson in 1907. Watercombe, another Thomas Baker house, has a summerhouse, roofed with Roman fish-scale tiles taken from a villa at Lillyhorn.

Bitton (8). The best church in the Bristol Quarter, made famous in the nineteenth century by the parsons Ellacombe, father and son, who were ninety-nine years vicar between them. The father was an authority on

Nether Lypiatt Manor, BISLEY

church bells, and his son wrote books on gardening. They made a collection of plants and the father listed over two thousand as early as 1831. Beautiful trees survive in the churchyard. The church is Saxon in origin, with Saxon sculpture above the chancel arch carved with the feet of a large rood. The Saxon nave was higher, and the existing hammerbeam roof was designed by the younger Ellacombe. On the north is a chantry chapel, *c.* 1300, with six lancet windows. The marvellous tower is Perpendicular, so is the vaulted chancel. The Ellacombes' vicarage has been sold complete with inscriptions, one with advice "to my successor" by H. T. Ellacombe, 1835. The new vicarage was built in glaring red brick with a clumsy concrete porch. There were copper and brass mills in Bitton in the nineteenth century; they made pans and dishes chiefly for the African market.

Blaisdon (2). On the edge of Dean. Blaisdon plum orchards. Roman Catholic Salesian school in Victorian mansion with park. Church, 1869, by Kempson of Hereford.

Blakeney (5). Has had a lot of through-traffic. Church rebuilt in 1820 with huge windows and ridiculous little tower.

Bledington (15). A church of unusual quality which owes its character to its position in the great stone belt, and the extraordinarily high standard of mason-craft available there in the fifteenth century. The north wall has a clerestory but no aisle. The windows have image niches with nodding ogee canopies in the splays, and brilliant fifteenth-century glass.

Blockley (12). The big village where once were silk mills. Stone-built on the side of the hill, with a long High Street. Church has a Norman chancel, once vaulted. Gothic-survival tower by the Woodwards of Chipping Campden. Monuments include a brass of a priest in full Mass vestments, and busts by Rysbrack of the owners of Northwick Park, a house enlarged by Lord Burlington in 1730, with further alterations before 1778

BLEDINGTON

by John Woolfe. The forcefulness of Burlington's work shows the mature architect at his best. His classically unified design for the east front deliberately retains the Jacobean gables to give picturesque attraction. The famous Northwick collection of pictures is now dispersed.

Boddington (13). In the vale near Cheltenham, church built on clay, hence the constant need for restoration; long low nave with scraped walls. The Manor, remodelled in Tudor style with battlements, stands

in a park. Some of the farmhouses and cottages are timber-framed.

Bourton-on-the-Hill (12). A long street running up steep hill with houses either side, now the road from Moreton-in-the-Marsh to Broadway. The Horse and Groom Inn sets the tone and scale with its Georgian ashlar front. At the bottom is Bourton House finished in the early eighteenth century on Tudor foundations and with a great barn built in 1570. The church looks Perpendicular from the outside, but has Norman

51

features inside. Outside the village training stables had been built by 1824.

Bourton-on-the-Water (15). The special character derives from the clear water of the river Windrush passing under low stone-built footbridges through broad grass verges, dotted with trees. The special attractions are the model village and Birdland. There are also some noteworthy buildings. The church has a Georgian tower with a dome, and fourteenth-century chancel; the rest is by Sir Thomas Jackson with a most beautiful coloured ceiling by F. E. Howard, and windows by Kempe. Harrington House is typical of *c.* 1740, and has some rococo plaster-work within.

Boxwell (16). Manor house (the home of the Huntley family since the Reformation) and church with a massive thirteenth-century bellcote,

down a long drive through boxwoods.

Brimpsfield (13). Manor belonged to the fierce Giffards till one of them seized some provision wagons belonging to Edward II as they proceeded along nearby Ermine Street. He was executed in Gloucester, and his castle at Brimpsfield, five years later, was reported to be "fallen down", and so it has remained to this day. The church has an attractive central tower, and there is no east window. It is a high-up place, 800 feet.

Bristol (8). *See p.* 121.

Broadwell (15). Tympanum with Maltese Cross. Table-tombs in churchyard, one with kneeling figures. A good stone village with a house by Guy Dawber, a village green, a ford, and farmhouses, barns and cottages.

The Manor next the church is Georgian.

Brockworth (13). Exceptionally interesting group of old buildings now submerged in suburbs of Gloucester. The Court was partly built by the last Prior of Lanthony, the Barn is probably fifteenth century and has nine bays with crucks, and the church has a central Norman tower with bold chevron mouldings on the arches. Seventeenth-century monument with bust.

Bromsberrow (2). Church has timber-framed belfry with a nineteenth-century shingled spire. There is a Georgian mortuary chapel with nice wrought-iron gates. Windows by Kempe. Bromsberrow Place is eighteenth century, altered with the Neo-Greek revival.

Brookthorpe (6). Under the Cots-

CHELTENHAM

wold scarp next a partly timber-framed house, a small mainly thirteenth-century church. Note the architect Detmar Blow's name carved, in good light, on the splay of a window.

Buckland (11). Church contains many treasures; fifteenth-century glass, seventeenth-century seating and gallery, Opus Anglicanum, a mazer bowl, and medieval tiles. The manor, close to, has been mostly rebuilt but the rectory is pre-Reformation and has a fifteenth-century open hall and stained glass.

Bulley (3). Norman church with rebuilt chancel; the alternate use of different coloured sandstones is well contrived.

Bussage (16). On a very steep hill. Church built in 1846 with the subscriptions of Oxford undergraduates, and a south aisle added a little later and designed by Bodley.

Cainscross (6). Church originally built in the 1830s but altered in the 1890s. Mills: one at Ebley, surprisingly by Bodley.

Cam (6). Mill founded in 1815 is the one cloth mill still working in the Cam valley, making smooth-faced cloth suitable for uniforms and billiard tables. Lower Cam church was designed by the vicar in 1844. Upper Cam church has a tower rebuilt it is said by the Lord Berkeley of the time of Edward II's murder. The vicarage, which appears in low relief on top of a tablet to the vicar who died in 1837, and the school, were designed the year before; "Gothic" but very symmetrical.

Chaceley (10). A good church though the walls of aisle and chancel are scraped. Unusual Norman chancel arch. Chaceley Hall is fifteenth century of close-studded timber-framing.

Chalford (6). Nonconformist chapels, handsome Georgian clothiers' houses and mills in the Golden Valley. Church built in 1724 with a classical arcade on the north, altered at differ-

ent times in the nineteenth century, and furnished by the Arts and Crafts Movement.

Charfield (5). Old church left in ruins as redundant churches should be.

Charlton Abbots (14). An over-restored little church and a handsome Jacobean manor house.

Charlton Kings (14). Suburb of Cheltenham. Several Regency houses survive, but infilling is spoiling the place. Battledown is a later development. Glenfall was altered c. 1923 by Sidney Barnsley, and has modelled plaster-work. The parish church is cruciform with central vaulted tower, and rebuilt chancel guarded by a life-sized marble angel. Holy Apostles is one of Middleton's five Cheltenham churches in High Victorian Decorated style.

Chedworth (14). A large straggling village, high up, with half a "wool" church at the prettier end. The setting of the Roman Villa in Chedworth woods is so romantic and beautiful that it almost cancels the

THE LODGE

10

Priory Street, CHELTENHAM

shock received by the unsuspecting visitor who finds that the only building above ground is a Victorian museum. However, some mosaic floors survive, and with a little imagination one can form a very good idea of what the house of a British landowner was like during the Roman occupation.

Cheltenham (14). In this *Shell Guide*, first published in 1939, Anthony West wrote hopefully: "Cheltenham is now aware of its beauty." This no doubt remains true, but the ingredients have not been properly understood. It was a carefully landscaped town. Much thought went into Papworth's layouts for Mont-

pellier and Lansdown, while at Rosehill he planted trees with the views of the Cotswolds in mind. No detail was ever left to chance in his search for perfect scale and proportion. This was the mood of all the creators of Cheltenham. How subtle is the calculated perspective of the Promenade, which is double the width at its upper end to what it is at its lower end. It is still one of the most beautiful towns in England; but the most terrible risks are being taken. It seems almost incredible that the Priory should have been demolished, a house faced in the most superb ashlar from Leckhampton quarry with fine carved details, and where the great Duke of Wellington stayed, and situated as the visually vital stop to the view of Priory Parade and Oxford Parade. Another risk seems

p. 56 Bayshill Road, CHELTENHAM
p. 57 Municipal Offices,
The Promenade

to be the introduction of modern buildings into the heart of the Regency town in Oriel Road, and the proposed destruction of that pretty house Oriel Lodge. These details, however, are insignificant when compared with the plans for the inner ring road, and the already existing and overwhelming visual insult, a skyscraper between the Bath Road and Vittoria Walk. This building is so big that it dominates everything and Cheltenham's visual uniqueness has gone for ever. To employ Geoffrey Jellicoe to lay out a new Greek Olympia for recreation, and to preserve certain sections of the town like Lansdown and Pittville, and to remove the bus station from the

Lansdown Place, CHELTENHAM

Queens Parade and Christchurch,
CHELTENHAM

Royal Crescent though excellent
ideas in themselves, are really not
enough if Cheltenham is to be pre-
vented from becoming commonplace.

HISTORY

There is an Iron Age camp on
Leckhampton Hill overlooking the
town. There are no Roman remains.
Cheltenham is Saxon in origin. The
Saxons settled on the plains and
chose sandy places for their homes.
Cheltenham sands are suitable to
build on; but where there is only
clay for foundations there is a constant maintenance problem. Both
contingencies are found contiguously,
and a geological survey is to be
recommended before buying property
in the town. At the time of the
Domesday Book, Reinbald the priest
is recorded as being in possession of
a holding at Cheltenham. He was
Chancellor to Edward the Confessor,
and founder of a college of canons at
Cirencester. The church property
remained in the hands of Cirencester's mitred Abbot till the Reformation—the manor belonged to
the Abbey of Fêcamp till 1414, and
afterwards to the Abbess of Syon.
Practically no medieval buildings
have survived, except the parish
church. The original town consisted
solely of the High Street. During the
Civil War, John Dutton of Sherborne
was Lord of the Manor. He was one
of many Royalists who were willing
to compound for confiscated estates,
and in fact eventually developed a
friendship with Cromwell. Cheltenham suffered little. Modern history,
however, really only begins with the
discovery of a spring possessing
purgative properties in 1718. This
became the Royal Old Well, and the
Spa was well and truly started, a
paradise for speculators gambling
on the over-indulgence of the Georgian upper-classes. The Royal Family
came for a five-week holiday in 1788,
which made Cheltenham fashionable
as a summer resort. In 1801 the
population was 3,000, rising to
20,000 in 1826. The architectural
vogue of the period was Greek revival, a style well suited by the cream-
coloured ashlar dug out of Leck-

Suffolk Square, CHELTENHAM

Number 3, Suffolk Square,
CHELTENHAM

hampton hill. Or if the houses should
be built of brick, also local, they could
just as easily be stuccoed over and
given that clear crisp look essential
for the pure classical style. Lightness
and elegance were introduced by the
wrought-iron and cast-iron balconies. When, after the Napoleonic
wars, foreign travel became prac-
ticable, people began going to con-
tinental watering-places, and the
lodging houses of Cheltenham became permanent residences, often
for retired civil servants and army
officers from India. At the same time
it became a centre for education with
good schools for boys and girls, and
a stronghold of evangelicalism (see
Anthony Trollope's *Miss Mackenzie*),
owing to the powerful personality
of the vicar, Francis Close.

The chief architects of Cheltenham
were:

John (Buonarotti) Papworth, worked in Cheltenham 1824–30, and
designed the layout of Lansdown
and Montpellier, the Rotunda, Lansdown Place and Crescent, and the
original Rosehill, besides the proto-
types for many small villas, and the
roof and pews of St James's Church,
Suffolk Square.

John Forbes designed the Pittville
Pump Room in 1825–30, and St
Paul's Church, 1827–31.

G. A. Underwood, assistant in Sir
John Soane's office, 1807–15, designed Holy Trinity Church, 1820–3,
and the Masonic Hall at the same
time, both in Portland Street. He
died in 1829 aged 36.

R. W. and C. Jearrad, brothers
who took over the speculator Thompson's enterprises in 1830, dismissing
Papworth. Therefore to them must
be given the very considerable credit
for Lansdown Terrace, besides the
Queen's Hotel, 1838, and Christ
Church, 1838–40.

Samuel Onley, active between 1847
and 1862. Houses in Bayshill.

W. H. Knight. Designer of Montpellier Walk *c.* 1840 with terra-cotta
caryatids by Rossi, and the synagogue
in St James's Square, 1837–9.

S. W. Daukes, Designed St Peter's
Church in successful Neo-Norman

Montpellier Walk, CHELTENHAM

style between 1847 and 1849, and St Paul's College, 1849.

John Middleton. Five churches counting Holy Apostles, Charlton Kings. All Saints, Pittville, the best, 1868. Delicious iron-work by his partner Prothero. St Mark, 1862–7. St Philip, Leckhampton, 1870. St Stephen, Tivoli, 1873. His son J. H. Middleton altered Christ Church, c. 1888.

SOME OF THE MANY GOOD GEORGIAN
AND LATER STREETS AND
BUILDINGS OF CHELTENHAM,
NOT ALREADY MENTIONED

South of the High Street

Cheltenham College: 1841, by J. Wilson of Bath, with additions by D. J. Humphris, J. Middleton, and the chapel by H. A. Prothero, 1896.

Thirlestaine House: 1823, by J. R. Scott in the best Neo-Greek style.

Ladies College: 1854. Additions by Middleton, 1876, Prothero, 1889, and the Princess Hall by E. R. Robson, 1896.

Municipal Offices: a terrace of c. 1823, as good as anything anywhere of this date.

Imperial Square: c. 1834. Stucco, cast-iron "double-heart" balconies.

Promenade Terrace: pairs of houses with pseudo-Corinthian capitals or Prince of Wales feathers. Clarence House is detached and intimate.

Montpellier Gardens: statue of William IV by "one of the rude sons of art, a self-taught stone-mason". (New Guide to Cheltenham, 1834.)

Lansdown Court: Italianate villas. 1830.

Lansdown Parade: ashlar fronts and Greek Doric porches.

Lypiatt Terrace: later Italianate.

Suffolk Square: c. 1825.

Montpellier Parade: Papworth-type villas. Regent Hotel was designed by him for Pearson Thompson. Claremont Lodge was originally built c. 1800, with additions, including the blank windows over the colonnaded porch with its four little bull's-eye windows, after 1834.

Vittoria Walk: Vittoria House was the first spa of Thompson's father

above CHERINGTON

below Nagshead between
CHERINGTON and AVENING

opened in 1804. Here and in Trafalgar Street are the cottages which smart society people rented when *rus in urbe* was the fashion; there is even a cottage ornée built of coloured vermiculated rocks and shells. How precious these survivors ought to be, for here Nelson's Captain Hardy stayed and there the Prince Regent was entertained—but it is there that an incongruous and enormous block of offices has been allowed.

Oriel Place: terrace 1825.

Oxford Buildings and Priory Buildings: in existence by 1820. Pretty wrought-iron window guards or verandas.

Priory Place: a cul-de-sac with some cottages shown on the 1826 map.

Bayshill Road: houses mostly by Samuel Onley.

Fauconberg House, 1847. Still Greek.

Overton Road: Abbeyholme built by John Middleton in 1865 in French-Gothic style, something quite new for domestic architecture in Cheltenham.

Royal Crescent: the earliest terrace, 1806–10.

The Park: 1833–9.

North of the High Street

St Margarets Terrace: before 1825. Magnificent wrought-iron balcony.

North Place: Countess of Huntingdon's chapel.

Pittville: estate developed in the early 1820s by Joseph Pitt who in 1812 was described as follows: "Pitt used to hold gentlemen's horses for a penny, when, appearing a sharp lad, an attorney at Cirencester took a fancy to him and bred him to his own business. He soon scraped together a little money by his practise in the law, and by degrees entered into speculation. . . . Everything has thriven with him. He has now a clear estate of £20,000 a year. . . ." The same year he became Member of Parliament for Cricklade. The Pittville Pump Room, 1825–30, was designed by John Forbes who had been trained at the Royal Academy School, entering in 1815 at the age of twenty. It has a great colonnade of Ionic columns taken from Stuart and Revett's engravings of the Temple of Ilissus. The interior is particularly beautiful with elliptical arches and pendentives on fluted

columns supporting a gallery with further pendentives beneath the dome, all richly encrusted with paterae and Greek patterns. It is the culmination of the superb landscape gardening of Pittville, Clarence Square and Wellington Square: Neo-Greek and Tudor-Gothic.

Cherington (16). Church has an unspoiled Early English chancel, and a sculptured Norman tympanum on the north—the one from the south is now over a doorway at Cherington Park. The small village has several nice Georgian cottages.

Chipping Campden (12). A Cotswold "wool" town in the Middle Ages. The merchant William Grevel's house still survives with its great bay window; he died in 1401. Till the coming of the motor the town remained remote and peaceful—it had received many benefactions from Sir Baptist Hicks in the seventeenth century, and in 1902 C. R. Ashbee's Guild of Handicrafts moved here, bringing a community of over a hundred people from London. The Campden Trust was formed in 1929 by F. L. Griggs who built a house here. Various properties in the High Street were bought and restored, and much of the character of the street may be a modern creation. The splendid Perpendicular church, like Northleach, appears to be all of one piece, though this is not exactly so. The arcades have remarkable deeply concave mouldings on piers and capitals, and the east window of the clerestory over the chancel arch is also a local characteristic. The lectern is a fifteenth-century latten eagle. There is Opus Anglicanum, a fine collection of wool merchants' memorial brasses, and the tomb of Viscount and Viscountess Campden by Joshua Marshall with standing effigies in shrouds. Adjacent to the churchyard are the lodges and gateway of the great house built by Sir Baptist Hicks in 1613, with their ogee-shaped ashlar roofs and central pediment. On a terrace in the field behind are the ruins of two pavilions with Renaissance motifs and twisted chimney stacks. Hicks was busy building Campden House in London at the same time. His country house did not

63

CHIPPING CAMPDEN Market Hall

survive the Civil War; but his Alms-houses did, and remain one of the most delightful buildings of the period in Gloucestershire.

The Roman Catholic church has a good stained glass window by Paul Woodroffe, 1909.

At Broad Campden is a small church by Prichard of Llandaff, 1868, with a communion rail by Ashbee, 1913; also a house made from a derelict Norman chapel by Ashbee. At Westington the Quarry is still worked; medieval manor and dovecote.

Churcham (13). Church spire rebuilt in 1878, a copy of the spire at Sompting; otherwise over-restored Norman.

Churchdown (13). Three churches for the suburbs between Cheltenham and Gloucester. Old church on the sky-line of Chosen Hill, an outlier of the

CHIPPING CAMPDEN Almshouses

Cotswolds near Gloucester; Norman and Early English. St Andrew, 1903 but nineteenth century in character, and St John, 1957 in the Regency style of Papworth, skilfully adapted by D. Stratton-Davis.

Cinderford (2). Plenty of ecclesiastical buildings for the miners of the Forest of Dean. Three churches. St John, 1844, by Edward Blore; a preaching church. St Stephen, 1890, by Lingen-Barker, and St Michael, Soudley, 1910. Wesley Chapel, 1849, more elaborate than the C of E. Baptist, 1860, Neo-classical.

Cirencester (17) Founded by the Romans as a fort for the army A.D. 43–60, but by the end of the century it was a town to become their second largest in the British Isles, and the centre of a very rich area full of villas. Excavations now continue annually whenever the opportunity

arises, and there is an excellent Corinium Museum. The small post-Roman Museum contains a few finds from the one and only excavation of the medieval abbey. The town has been controlled planning-wise hitherto by the two great private estates of Abbey and Park which almost touch in the middle. The former is now being developed for the public benefit but the latter with its great rides originally planted in the early eighteenth century remains mercifully inviolate. Visually the dominating feature is the Perpendicular church tower, built *c.* 1399 at the west end of the grandest "wool" church in England. The influence of the Abbot predominated in medieval times, and as he held a monopoly of the wool, the townspeople were hardly able even to form a trade guild. The church received its final form just before the Reformation, when the nave arcades were rebuilt. The upper-storeyed porch belonged to the Abbot who used it as an office for treating with the King's Commissioners. It later became the Town Hall, and has only comparatively recently served parochial purposes. Of the many other features of the church which are of special interest, mention must be made of the beautiful open-work Perpendicular parapets round the east end and north chapel, the angel corbels bearing the shields of the donors of the roof of the nave, the wooden screens (Midland style with bands of open quatrefoils), the medieval glass in the east window and western-most window of the south aisle, the Hardman glass in St John's chapel and elsewhere, the fan-vaults in St Catherine's chapel, the stone screen and brasses in the Trinity chapel, the monuments in the Lady chapel, and Queen Anne Boleyn's cup and cover, given later to Dr Master, and now exhibited in the nave as a memorial to his descendant.

After the wool period came a time of prosperity for the clothiers; but when that declined with the Industrial Revolution, there was little left in the way of business for the inhabitants of Cirencester except what came with the stage-coaches. Stagna-

tion during the nineteenth century has luckily preserved the medieval streets, and many houses of the Elizabethan, Jacobean and Georgian periods, such as Cotswold Lodge, for example, with its fine Renaissance chimneypiece. Apart from a few light industries the recent well-being of the town is based on the agriculture of the district, and the presence of the Royal Agricultural College. The Urban District Council is now conscious of its architectural heritage. After the disastrous development in Dyer Street great efforts have successfully been made to preserve the character of Gloucester Street. It is to be hoped this is a good augury for the intact preservation of the conservancy areas in the town.

Clapton-on-the-Hill (15). Very small

mostly Norman church. Latin indulgence, of the most liberal terms, inscribed on the chamfered abacus of the northern respond of the chancel arch. Strawberries are grown here commercially.

Clearwell (5). The Castle was built in about 1735, and is therefore one of the oldest Georgian Gothic houses in England. The architecture is of classical discipline yet authentically medieval in feeling. The splendid church is by John Middleton, 1866.

Coaley (6). Elm country on the edge of the Vale below Dursley. Church rebuilt in the 1850s except the Perpendicular tower.

Coates (17). Beautiful Early Perpen-

BROAD CAMPDEN church

dicular church tower. Three-bay Transitional south arcade. Generally of above average interest. Houses and cottages by Barnsley and Jewson. Eighteenth - century canal maintenance men's houses on the Thames–Severn Canal, and also in the parish the entrance to the Canal Tunnel, and the source of the Thames marked by a statue of Neptune, reclining uncomfortably in the far from lush Cotswold grass, and perhaps regretting his almost forgotten life in the Crystal Palace.

Coberley (14). Although the church's nave and chancel were rebuilt by John Middleton *c.* 1870, it remains a building of exceptional interest because of the south chapel with its quatrefoil lowside window decorated with ballflower, the Decorated tracery in the other windows, the effigies of the Berkeley Knight who fought at Crécy and his wife and others, including a heart-burial, the south doorway and the Perpendicular tower.

Cold Ashton (9). Church entirely rebuilt at the beginning of the sixteenth century by Thomas Key whose punning rebus appears in many places. The Manor was built for a Mayor of Bristol *c.* 1629. Another large house at some distance is Battlefields, named after the Battle of Lansdown in 1643 (where Sir Bevil Granville was killed) Georgian Gothic by C. Harcourt Masters, 1802. Hamswell is also in the parish. This is an old house remodelled in the early eighteenth century.

Coleford (5). In a shed in the garden of Forest House David Mushet first produced good cast steel. Late Georgian terrace houses, the tower of an 1821 church, Congregational chapel 1842, still classical, a Baptist chapel in Romanesque style of the 1850s, a Town Hall rebuilt in 1866, uninteresting municipal, a new church of 1880, and a magistrates' court, fire station, and police station from the County Architect's Department of the 1950s.

Colesbourne (14). The shade of Henry Elwes lingers on in the park, amongst his trees and lakes; but the mansion by David Brandon has mostly gone. The little church nearby is cruciform with a western tower; chalice-shaped pulpit. Victoriana include windows by the two Ws, Wailes and Willement, a Kempe east window, and some nice needlework. Five bells by Abraham Rudhall, 1719. The inn on the main road was curiously built of quartz and tufa, in 1827.

Coln Rogers (14). The nave and chancel of the Saxon church have survived almost intact except that the chancel has been lengthened, and a tower has been built in the west end of the nave. Saxon features to recognize are the flat pilaster strips with small stepped bases, the long-and-short quoins, and the window on the north made from a single stone. The south doorway is Norman, so is the font. Fifteenth-century fragmented figure of St Margaret in north window of nave. The arched doorway of a priest's house survives in the farmyard to the west.

Coln St Aldwyns (18). An attractive village by the river between great estates. The gabled manor was the house of a Victorian Chancellor of the Exchequer, Sir Michael Hicks-Beach. His descendant Lord St Aldwyn lives in a square Georgian house in Williamstrip Park. Coln church is over-restored inside, but the tower is fine with Norman work at the bottom, Early English in the middle and Perpendicular on top. Inscribed on the step of the Font is a palindrome in Greek. John Keble's father was vicar here.

Coln St Dennis (14). Delightful situation in the Coln Valley. Norman church of unaltered plan; the flat Norman buttresses survive at both east and west ends, and the central tower is Norman except for the top. The shafts for the springing of a stone vault remain in the small chancel, but the chancel arch has been rebuilt as the result of a failure when the tower was heightened.

Compton Abdale (14). The best thing about the church is its situation in this high Cotswold hamlet, and its

In CIRENCESTER Park

tower, which is Perpendicular and has sculptures.

Compton Greenfield (8). Over-restored Norman church; off the beaten track.

Condicote (15). A high-up North Cotswold place with a village green enclosed by dry-stone walls, and with a fourteenth-century wayside cross. At each corner is a farmhouse, forming a nucleus for many acres. The Norman church has been over-restored, and has a scraped interior. Hinchwick Manor was designed by C. R. Cockerell in 1826 as a rather grand farm house.

Corse (3). Snigs End was established in 1847 by Feargus O'Connor, the Chartist, as a settlement on the land for industrial workers. Corse church and Court are in another dead-end; the church is simple with a broach spire, and the house is also ancient and has cruck-trusses.

Cowley (14). The mansion is now used by the county for good works and public occasions; it was rebuilt *c.* 1860, by Somers-Clarke in Italian-palace style, and enlarged later, by simply adding more and more similar bays. The tiny church alongside is thirteenth century, with lancet windows, and a Perpendicular top stage to the tower.

Cranham (13). Hilly village next to large areas of beechwoods. The church's Perpendicular tower is enlivened by carved pairs of sheep-shears. It possesses a pre-Reformation screen, which is a rare thing in the Gloucester diocese, since Bishop Hooper was only too successful in securing the destruction of most of them. It also has a small collection of rustic Baroque stone monuments with putti holding palms and trumpets which are made of wood.

Cromhall (5). The medieval church has interesting features but the outside is aesthetically dull. The north doorway has a Decorated ogee tre-foiled arch, and an original door, and the door on the south is also ancient. Chalice-shaped stone pulpit. Tablets

by the usual local masons including Paty, King of Bath, and Daw of Berkeley; a new one by Bryant Fedden.

Cutsdean (11). High and remote north Cotswold hamlet with a poor church rebuilt in 1863.

Daglingworth (17). A comfortable place on the Churn just above Cirencester. The Saxon features of the church include three well-preserved sculptures in the nave and north aisle, a small crucifix high up on the outside of the east end, and a sundial over the south doorway. The door itself is late fifteenth century. On the north side of the chancel is a reset Norman stone altar. The high altar and reredos were designed by W. H. Randoll Blacking in 1957, and

Cruck construction, DIDBROOK

the Victorian figures in the east window were made to float in clear glass; a practice to be deprecated though the effect of light on lime-washed walls, as seen through the low chancel arch, is beautiful. The dovecote at the Manor is medieval, circular, and still has a potence or revolving ladder.

Daylesford (15). S. P. Cockerell built the house here for Warren Hastings, but not in the Indian style like Sezincote. Some can see a Muslim twist to the dome, and a fireplace certainly sports Hindu women. Many of Hastings' possessions have returned to the house, including Stubbs' picture of his yak roaming the park. There is now a lake with a polythene bottom and an illusory island. Hastings' tomb is

Crucifixion, DAGLINGWORTH

71

made of Coade stone and it is just east of the church he rebuilt, but the existing church is yet another rebuilding by J. L. Pearson and it has a marvellous dark High Church interior with Clayton & Bell's very best windows.

Deerhurst (10). The priory church dates from the eighth or ninth century, and was restored in the tenth after the Viking invasions. The western porch was made into a tower, and an apsidal chancel (now ruinous) rebuilt. The earliest chapels, or porticuses as they are called, are still separated from the central space by walls with doorways at two levels; but the later ones further west have been opened to the nave by cutting very good Early English arcades. Saxon sculptures include the eighth-century Virgin and Child, and a tenth - century Byzantine-looking Angel *in situ* on the apse. The font is also dateable—late ninth century, decorated with double trumpet-spiral ornament. Later features of interest are the fourteenth-century stained glass figure of St Catherine, the seating arrangement in the sanctuary, which is Puritan, and the brass to Sir John Cassey *c.* 1400, whose wife has a dog called Terri. Nearby Odda's Chapel is also Saxon. There is con-

clusive evidence that it was dedicated by Earl Odda in honour of the Holy Trinity in 1056.

Didbrook (11). A delightful church with plenty of light to see the way the west tower is carried on arches within the nave. A Georgian chancel arch survived the Victorian restorers. Medieval glass in the east window. A much photographed cruck cottage in the village.

Didmarton (9). The old church of St Lawrence retains some Georgian furnishings including a three-decker pulpit. It is in fact a medieval church unaltered since the eighteenth century, because the Victorians (in the shape of T. H. Wyatt) built a new church in the village, instead of restoring the old one.

Dodington (9). One of Gloucestershire's three largest stately homes. Built by James Wyatt, between 1796 and 1816, for Bethell Codrington whose family had made a fortune in the West Indies. Apart from the hexastyle portico which has a Grecian flavour, the house is Roman in inspiration and detail. The fashionable curved conservatory, with a picture gallery behind, joins the mansion on to the church, which is

cruciform and domed. The romantic setting was picturesque enough even before Capability Brown added the final touch with his Gothic cascade, and it must have been Codrington who insisted on Roman architecture rather than Gothic. The Dower House, now used as a private house by the family, was built as a Roman bath-house cum dairy where the ladies could make butter. There is a good rotunda of a lodge on the Bath road near the M4.

Dowdeswell (14). A beautiful place on the Cotswold edge outside Cheltenham. An inscription states that the central tower had its spire rebuilt in 1577. The galleries survive, one for the manor, and another in the north transept for the rectory, both approached as so many were, by private external doors and staircases. There is a priest's brass on the floor of the chancel, *c.* 152•, and a delightful Baroque monument by Christopher Horsnaile, of 1734, with a bust of William Rogers. Next the churchyard are several farm buildings of Tudor origin. The Court, built in 1834, has lost its top storey. Upper Dowdeswell is Elizabethan, and later. Sandywell Park was originally built *c.* 1700. Horace Walpole's cousin Lord Conway (later Lord Hertford) lived here

DODINGTON

DUNTISBOURNE ROUSE

and may have added the Gibbs style wings, after Walpole is said to have derided it—"a square box of a house, very dirtily situated".

Down Ampney (17). A village on the Wiltshire border in flat upper Thames water-meadows, where Vaughan-Williams was born in 1872. The church has a conspicuous fourteenth-century spire. Inside, the north arcade is Transitional with cylindrical piers and pointed arches, the soffits of which are painted with red flowers with white centres. The screen to the north transept incorporates Jacobean work; but most of the elaborate furnishings are by Ponting, 1898 onwards. Decorated fourteenth-century tomb with effigies; also two seventeenth-century kneeling effigies of Hungerford knights whose house

survives on the west. It has an open medieval hall, and a front doorway designed by Sir John Soane in 1799. The Tudor gatehouse was demolished in 1963.

Down Hatherley (3). Rebuilt church and rectory in the Decorated style of Fulljames and Waller. Possesses one of Gloucestershire's nine lead fonts though this one is Tudor. Underneath the unpromising brick front of Hatherley Court there hides a seventeenth-century stone house with contemporary staircase, modelled plaster ceilings, panelling and chimneypieces, besides a Regency drawing-room.

Doynton (8). In the Bristol quarter where Pennant stone is sometimes used. The heavily restored church

has herringbone masonry which is post-Conquest. Gothic survival tower 1644. Several houses are built with conspicuous relieving arches over the windows.

Driffield (17). Church rebuilt in 1734 by Lord Coleraine whose family tablets include one to the Regency rake who died in 1824: "He lived and died a firm believer in One God and in One God only. He was also a practical Christian as far as his frail nature did allow him to be so." The church now, however, has a nineteenth-century Tractarian atmosphere due to the influence of Butterfield, and the complete set of Alexander Gibbs windows.

Drybrook (2). Holy Trinity Church, 1817. Preaching church. East window

DURSLEY

by J. C. N. Bewsey, a brilliant stained-glass artist who came to a tragic end.

Dumbleton (11). The Hall was designed by George S. Repton in Tudor style in 1830. It has a good view over its park; at the gates is a church with interesting monuments to the Cocks family, including a bust by Peter Bennier, 1654. Churchyard: well-preserved eighteenth-century headstones in low-relief.

Duntisbourne Abbots (14). A pretty village with the mostly Norman but over-restored church standing centrally on a sloping site. Some distance away is Cotswold Farm, a house enlarged by Sidney Barnsley in 1926, and containing a window by Burne-Jones.

Duntisbourne Leer (14). A ford where the Churn runs across the road between farmhouse and cottages.

DURSLEY: market house

Duntisbourne Rouse (14). Small church with Saxon nave, and probably slightly later chancel where it was possible to take advantage of the steep slope and build a crypt underneath with a Norman window and tunnel vault. The tiny tower has the upper stage dated 1587 and a saddle-back roof. Pinbury Park is in the parish, set overlooking the hanging beech woods of the Frome valley. It belonged to the nuns of Caen and then to the Abbess of Syon, hence the Nuns Walk, a splendid avenue of yews. It is also noted as the home of the county historian Sir Robert Atkyns who died in 1711, and more recently of Ernest Gimson the brilliant interpreter of the Arts and Crafts Movement who died in 1919.

Dursley (8). Market town at the foot of the Cotswold escarpment with a market house of 1738 bearing a statue of Queen Anne. Ancient streets meet here but many old houses have been demolished in recent years. A great part of the church is

built of tufa which is quarried nearby; it is medieval, restored by Sir T. G. Jackson. The tower was rebuilt in Gothic-survival style in 1709. Inside, note the excessively stilted arches of the fifteenth-century arcades, the Tanner chapel, the east window by Burlison and Grylls, and the baptistry by Randoll Blacking.

Dymock (2). The Norman church has a splendid south doorway with chevroned arch, Tree of Life tympanum, and tongued volute capitals, typical of the district. The interior is horribly scraped. Three-quarters of a mile to the north is Little Iddens, a timber-framed cottage where the American poet Robert Frost lived in 1914.

Dyrham (8). The mansion belongs to the National Trust. It is like two houses back to back. The earlier one facing west was built in 1692 by a French Huguenot architect Samuel Hauduroy for William Blathwayt when he was Secretary of State. The

75

ELKSTONE

scale is domestic and completely delightful. On the east side, which was added by Talman from 1698 to 1704, we have the grand façade, comparable with the south front of Chatsworth. The two portions are linked by Hauduroy's rebuilt great hall of the old house. The gardens were laid out in the Dutch manner by George London. Inside the house much of its original furniture is *in situ*, including the state bed which Blathwayt prepared to receive Queen Anne should she ever come. The church joins the house, and is mid-thirteenth century with a Perpendicular tower, fifteenth-century glass, monuments and brasses.

Eastington (6). Perpendicular church with south chapel added by Duke of Buckingham before his execution in 1521. Fragments of glass from this period survive with the Duke's initials, and there are lovely windows by Sir Ninian Comper and F. C. Eden. High Altar by Stephen Dykes-Bower. The churchyard is bounded by the river Frome on the south alongside the terrace wall of a former Elizabethan mansion, demolished in the eighteenth century. At Alkerton Grange is an early eighteenth-century gazebo built of brick with stone dressings and Baroque pediment.

Eastleach (15). Small village with two medieval churches, one either side of the river, and both of considerable interest. The church of Eastleach Turville has a notable thirteenth-century chancel with a quite elaborate triple lancet east end. The south doorway has a Norman tympanum of a Majesty within a vesica supported by angels. The church of Eastleach Martin, more often called Bouthrop, has a beautiful north transept added in the fourteenth century, and so here we have three fine Decorated windows comparatively rare in the Cotswolds. Note the cross-loop on the belfry stairs. Medieval benches at the back of the nave. Both churches have niches in the east walls of their

76

porches. Both are charming and picturesquely situated; but somehow Bouthrop with its oil lamps has a more completely countrified and un-restored atmosphere. A footbridge of flat paving stones crosses the river, called Keble's bridge, more likely in honour of earlier Kebles than John Keble who was non-resident curate after his ordination in 1815.

Ebrington (12). On the edge of the North Cotswolds; the village has a good group of cottages which still have thatched roofs. St Eadburga's church is partly Norman, with an over-restored thirteenth-century chancel having a very low east win-dow, filled with glass by Christopher Webb since 1964. Wall paintings, black-letter texts at west end, seven-teenth-century pulpit and lectern,

monument of a Lord Chief Justice, 1476, busts of Sir John and Lady Keyt, 1662, by Thomas Burman, and a Hoptonwood stone tablet with lettering by Eric Gill. The manor house dates from the thirteenth century but has been much altered at different times.

Edgeworth (14). Remains of Saxon church include the blocked north doorway half hidden by a chimney flue. The south doorway is rich Norman. Chancel Norman with three lancets added above the east window, Victorian rere-arches, and scraped walls. Some fifteenth-century bench-ends with poppy-head finials. Fourteenth-century glass depicting a bishop. Manor House, close by, is Queen Anne altered in 1899 by Sir Ernest George. Spectacular situation

with hanging beech woods in the valley.

Elberton (5). Church mostly Victorian but retains Decorated tower and spire. Jacobean manor with elaborate staircase.

Elkstone (14). One of the most famous of the Norman Cotswold churches, because of its exquisite little stone vaulted chancel and south doorway ornamented with beak-heads and containing a Majesty in the tym-panum. The fine tower is a Perpen-dicular addition. The priest's house contains remains of a wall painting; rectory early eighteenth century, altered in 1847.

Elmore (3). Gloucester Vale, black and white thatched cottages and cruck-framed barns. Elmore Court,

FAIRFORD

on land which has belonged to the same family since the thirteenth century, was built *c*. 1580, on a medieval site and has a Georgian wing. The entrance gates by William Edney date from before 1712, and are decorated with acanthus and hart's-tongue fern, and crowned by the swan badge of the Guise family, the prettiest gates in Gloucestershire. The churchyard contains some of the finest carved table tombs of Painswick stone, deeply undercut and full of imaginative invention.

Elmstone Hardwicke (13). In dull country just outside Cheltenham. The church has a Perpendicular tower retaining some imagery. Inside is a carved Saxon stone similar to the font at Deerhurst, but the most obvious feature is the huge stone reredos of 1886, with carved saints under crocketed canopies.

English Bicknor (2). Church built of a forest sandstone which has not lasted so that the unpromising appearance of the exterior gives no clue as to the splendid Norman work inside, arcades of unaltered twelfth-century piers with carved capitals and one arch with chevrons and beak heads. Long Early English chancel. Monuments.

Evenlode (12 & 15). Pretty straggling village near the county border at Four Shires Stone though Worcestershire has long since lost its right to be included. The church has archaeological interest only, except for the beautiful fifteenth-century carved oak pulpit, and the two-bay arcade of lozenge-shaped octagonal piers and pointed arches without capitals.

Fairford (18). The church was rebuilt in the high Perpendicular period, *c*. 1500, with an elaborate tower on old foundations. Famous throughout the country for its stained glass windows made for the church at the end of the fifteenth century by the shop of Henry VII's master glass painter Barnard Flower. They can be compared with those in King's College Chapel, Cambridge, from the same source. The subjects were

The orangery and canal,
Frampton Court,
FRAMPTON-ON-SEVERN

Frampton Court, FRAMPTON-ON-SEVERN

taken from one of the early printed books, illustrated with woodcuts, the *Biblia Pauperum*. The backgrounds show Flemish buildings as well as English Perpendicular architecture. The scheme endeavours to present the entire Catholic faith, beginning with Adam and Eve on the north side outside the lady chapel and ending with the great west window which is given up to the Last Judgement and, though more restored than the others, must always have a universal appeal, even if the devils do not haunt your imagination from Sunday to Sunday as was intended. Other features of outstanding interest are the brasses to the founder Tame and his family, and the screens round the chancel. The little town has not altered much for many years except for the proximity of the Fairford Aerodrome, large enough to take the Concorde, and it has lost its big house in favour of a school and there are new council houses; however, there is still a vicar called Keble living in Keble House.

Falfield (5). Eastwood Park was home of the Prime Minister, time of Waterloo. Small church by Daukes on the main road.

Farmcote (14). The nave of a Norman church. Interesting furnishings; two-decker pulpit, Laudian communion rails, Elizabethan effigies.

Farmington (15). Limestone quarries here are still worked. Church with Norman features notably the cylindrical piers of the arcade with their overhanging scalloped capitals, and the chevroned chancel and south door arches. Farmington Lodge is Georgian altered in 1854.

Filton (8). St Peter's church re-orientated and rebuilt in 1961, opposite the new buildings of the Bristol Aeroplane Co, now a part of Rolls-Royce and home of the Concorde project, with factories spreading across many acres lining the A38 to the north. Filton's assimilation into Bristol began with Sir George White's trams in 1908 and his aeroplanes in 1910, and increased with each war's expanded production. However it still retains vestiges of its village character, with a thriving community centre and excellent lending library.

Flaxley (2). Church rebuilt by Sir George Gilbert Scott in 1856, with a reredos by J. Birnie Philip. The Abbey House has remains of a Cistercian monastery founded in about 1150, consisting of a fine twelfth-century rib-vaulted undercroft and a fourteenth-century abbot's guest hall. In the seventeenth century rooms were remodelled over the refectory and have rudimentary Venetian-type windows, restored by

Oliver Messel in 1961–2. The south wing was added in 1777–83 by Anthony Keck, architect, of Kings Stanley, in the manner of Adam.

Forthampton (10). Village with seventeenth-century timber-framed thatched houses, one considerably older with an original hall. On the far side of the river Severn almost opposite Tewkesbury. Church retains a stone mensa but is over-restored. The former reredos, made in 1845 in poker-work by a curate, is preserved. Forthampton Court belonged to Tewkesbury Abbey. Abbot Wakeman retired here bringing with him a crusader's tomb, now in the garden. The house was altered by Philip Webb, in 1891. His staircase leads into the chapel where is a late thirteenth-century picture supposed always to have been here.

Framilode (6). St Peter's church built by Francis Niblett, 1854, in Romanesque style. Situated on the bank of the river Severn. There were mills for making iron-wire. Beginning of Stroudwater Canal, 1775.

Frampton Cotterell (8). Famous for manufacturing felt hats. St Peter's Church rebuilt by John Norton, 1858; Gothic revival.

Frampton Mansell (16). Neo-Norman church, 1844. Regular William and Mary farmhouse almost underneath

the railway arches. Pretty steep situation near Sapperton.

Frampton-on-Severn (5). The most interesting village in the Berkeley Vale, with houses either side of a wide green leading to a closer concentration of buildings and the church. Nearly all are old, and some timber-frames may be medieval. The big house on the left of the green is Frampton Court built between 1731 and 1733 probably by John Strahan of Bristol. It has a notable interior with joinery of the highest quality and condition. There is a canal, and an orangery in the Gothic style of William Halfpenny with delicious ogee arches. The church is mainly fourteenth century with fifteenth-century additions, and has one of the six similar lead fonts of 1250–75 surviving in the county. Good furnishings and monuments as well; note the tablet by John Pearce to his brothers. Fromebridge Mill, a quarter of a mile to the east, has old machinery still working. Canal house in Doric taste by Mylne or Telford, further west.

France Lynch (16). Near Chalford approached by steep and narrow lane with crowded cottages and Nonconformist chapels. Bodley's first church; French Gothic, and Ruskin.

Frenchay (8). Georgian houses round a green common on the outskirts of Bristol; the Manor House looks as if it was by the elder Wood of Bath. There is also a Unitarian Chapel built in 1720, a Friends' Meeting House in 1808, and a church of 1834 which has a mean Gothic appearance though the galleried interior is better.

Fretherne with **Saul** (6). Unspoiled Victorian (1847) church by Francis Niblett, enlarged ten years later. Quite elaborate. A poker-work picture by the curate of Forthampton. All windows (except one) by Rogers of Worcester, 1859. The house at Fretherne, called Luffinghams, is framed with four pairs of crucks,

GLOUCESTER:

above: Dock warehouses
below: The approach from the west

smoke-blackened in the roof, and has two newel staircases, arched door-heads, curved braces and ovolo-moulded mullions. Saul church has a Caen stone reredos from St Michael's, Gloucester, set in a rebuilt chancel. These places have several terraces of boatmen's cottages, with names like Prospect Place, 1852, Victoria Place, 1854, and Prince of Wales Terrace, 1863. One cottage has carved figures of twin sailors and doves.

Frocester (6). Frocester Court is on the site of a Roman villa, and is itself largely medieval. The tithe barn was built before 1306, and is one of the oldest and best preserved barns in England; some of the stone may be Roman in origin. Small rather dull church. Only the Victorian tower of the other demolished church survives.

Gloucester (3 & 13). The medieval city has almost completely disappeared. In fact the houses round the Cross have been rebuilt several times resulting in a most unworthy centre for any town anywhere; but Gloucester is also a cathedral city and an inland port. The Cathedral precinct, known as College Green, is a quiet oasis in spite of being partly a car park. The port is fed by Mylne and Telford's Gloucester–Berkeley Canal, 1827, and there are some big nineteenth-century warehouses. The Shire Hall in Westgate Street is by Sir Robert Smirke, 1816, and now has a vast great extension, 1966, eight storeys high and mostly of glass, joined to the older buildings and flying across Bearland Street. HM Prison lies between this and the harbour, on the site of Gloucester Castle. There is an old Custom House in Quay Street.

The *Cathedral* was begun in 1089 by the Norman Benedictine abbot Serlo. A fire in 1122 destroyed the wooden roof. By 1242 the stone vaulting of the nave was completed. The south aisle was rebuilt in 1318; the Norman vaulting survives only on the north. After the murder of Edward II at Berkeley Castle, his tomb became an object of pilgrimage, and therefore a source of revenue, and between 1331 and 1337 the Perpendicular style was born in the south transept. The first fan vaults also are to be found in the cloisters, 1351 to

GLOUCESTER Cathedral
p. 82: The choir
p. 83: The cloisters

1377. Perpendicular rebuilding continued during the whole of the period, with the remodelling of the presbytery, the erection of the vast east window, the tower *c.* 1450, and finally the lady chapel *c.* 1450–99, which was the last major alteration to the abbey, converted by Henry VIII into a cathedral in 1541. The second bishop was Hooper who was burnt in St Mary's Square in 1554 for his Protestant opinions. When William Laud was Dean, in 1616, High Church principles were observed, and the communion rails in the lady chapel are of this period. The cathedral was restored by Sir G. G. Scott; but came to no harm, in fact the encaustic tiles in the presbytery, and his reredos are admirable. For a more detailed description of the architecture of the cathedral, the reader is recommended to look at Vol. II of *Gloucestershire* in the "Buildings of England", Penguin Books. A few of the more interesting features, however, must be noted here. First observe the enormous cylindrical piers of the nave, a west country innovation not found elsewhere. Then see the splendid Perpendicular veil that is drawn over the Norman work in the presbytery, culminating in the magical glass wall at the east end and supporting almost invisibly the great stone vaulted roof covered in a hundred carved bosses. Note the lovely medieval glass in this window given after the Battle of Crécy. Walk round the ambulatory from where on the north side the best view of Edward II's shrine and effigy is obtained. Tier upon tier of little ogee arches, and crocketed pinnacles, rise above the crowned alabaster head with its long curled hair, resting upon a cushion supported by angels. The lady chapel, finished almost 200 years after the first Perpendicular building began and still in the same style, is gorgeous and colourful with a jumble of medieval glass in the east window, and Christopher Whall's glass in the rest. Here are the monuments by Samuel Baldwin to the two married daughters of Bishop Miles

Lanthony Priory, GLOUCESTER

The New Inn, GLOUCESTER

Smith the Puritan, who is said to have been so offended by Dean Laud he never set foot in the cathedral again. In the south transept is the monument of Alderman Blackleech who died in 1639, good quality English work of the period. There are lots of eighteenth-century tablets, one with sculptured figures by Flaxman, and of the later monuments the best is a bronze kneeling effigy of a priest by Henry Wilson, in memory of Canon Tinling.

On the east side of the cloisters is the chapter house where it is said William the Conqueror ordered the Domesday survey. The library above contains the Chapter Act Book of which the first Act is the decree of Dean Laud for the moving of the communion table to the upper end of the choir. The former Deanery (once the Norman abbot's lodging) has a panelled room known as the Laud Room, but with slightly earlier panelling. Renaissance in style, and similar to work at Red Lodge, Bristol.

GLOUCESTER Cathedral

There are two interesting monastic ruins in Gloucester both well restored by the Ministry of Works: Black Friars and Grey Friars. The former, one of three Dominican Friaries to have survived in England, was established in 1239, and existed till 1539 when it was given to a clothier. It has recently undergone a thorough process of de-secularization; but Grey Friars proved impossible to disentangle totally from a Georgian house. Other churches in Gloucester number nineteen, or twenty; the most interesting are St Mary de Crypt, mostly rebuilt in the fifteenth century; St Nicholas, with its pretty Perpendicular tower and spire; and St John the Baptist, eighteenth-century classical. For the rest, All Saints is by Sir G. G. Scott, St Barnabas is by Cachemaille-Day, 1939, and St Aldate is thoroughly modern, by Robert Potter and Richard Hare, 1964. The RC church of St Peter has a very good conspicuous spire.

The newest buildings in Gloucester are not unworthy and its changing face is beginning to be rather exciting. The Eastgate market, by Shingler, Risdon & Associates, provides dramatic effects particularly in relation to the historic buildings nearby such as Grey Friars, and a completely new view of St Mary de Crypt church. The County Council's restaurant on top of the Shire Hall also provides new views over the Cathedral City, and their delightful County Library replaces the old barracks opposite the prison.

Lanthony Priory. The site of the Augustinian priory, a daughter-house of Llanthony St John in the Monmouthshire mountains, is now nearly waste-land by the side of the Gloucester–Berkeley Canal. The ruins of a fourteenth-century gate-house, part of the tithe barn, and a timber-framed and stone building survive, but only just, and maybe not for much longer.

Gotherington (11). Countess of Huntingdon's chapel. Quite a growing new population.

Great Badminton (9). Seventeenth-century ducal mansion. Grinling Gibbons carvings in the dining room, *c.* 1683. Altered by William Kent, who added the pavilions, the twin wooden cupolas, and central pediment. The game of badminton was invented in the hall. Worcester Lodge, also by Kent, was designed in 1746 and is one of the most superb park buildings in England, containing a Palladian dining room over

below and opposite HIDCOTE

Lodge, HIGHNAM

the archway. Kent died two years later, and his successor Thomas Wright designed the castellated farm-buildings round about. Generally, however, the park is now more famous for the annual Horse Trials. The village has houses of all periods, and several thatched cottages ornées on the road to Acton Turville. Church attached to the house, was built in 1785; monuments by Grinling Gibbons, Rysbrack and R. Westmacott. Heraldic windows by Willement, chancel furnishings by Temple Moore.

Great Rissington (15). Church, rectory, manor and a farmhouse comprise the south-west corner of the village. The church is cruciform with central tower rising from the late twelfth-century arches of the crossing. Furnishings date mostly from 1939–40. The street, with widely spaced houses, runs up hill to a triangular green, and further the road divides round a four-sided green, before coming to the RAF Aerodrome.

Great Witcombe (13). Situated just below the Cotswold escarpment at Birdlip Hill, in a beautiful park-like bowl. The parish has scattered farms and cottages, the remains of quite a large Roman villa, and church with a Norman chancel arch, a fifteenth-century north aisle with nice Perpendicular windows, and an eighteenth-century tower and porch.

Gretton (11). Picture-book timber-framed cottages and tower of ruined medieval church; new church in the manner of Gilbert Scott by J. D. Wyatt.

Guiting Power (14). Guiting stone is now quarried only at Coscombe, which is nearer Stanway than Guiting. A pretty village but a lot of the houses have been over-restored and consequently lost their personality. It seems the deadly hand of a perfectionist has been at work. The Norman church has been much altered, with early nineteenth-century transepts. The restoration of 1903 provided corbel heads of the reigning monarchs. Guiting Grange is a stylish house of 1848, set in a nice little park.

Hailes (11). Goal of pilgrims; Cistercian abbey founded 1246, excavated by Ministry of Works and owned by National Trust. Finds housed in Museum. Church has medieval stained glass and wall-paintings, and unspoiled furnishings.

Ham and Stone (5). The church is at Stone, and is mostly thirteenth and fourteenth century with a spire. Situated in the Berkeley vale it is hardly surprising to find the Berkeley arms in the medieval glass, and an eighteenth-century tablet by Pearce of Frampton.

Hamfallow (5). Another flat place in the Berkeley vale with many hedge-row elm trees, but in this case there is not only no church but no village. There are, however, some pretty hamlets and farms. Breadstone is one of the former, with a medieval manor farm and an early Victorian residence nearby. The oldest house is Wanswell Court with its splendid hall of c. 1450. So good was its chimney-piece that the last Earl of Berkeley removed it to the hall of Berkeley Castle. Curious features in the parlour are original spyholes facing outdoors diagonally. Acton Hall is a late eighteenth-century brick-built house regular, pedimented and centrally Venetian windowed and Tuscan porticoed.

Hampnett (14). Norman church with vaulted sanctuary and small choir over which there must have been a tower. Existing tower fifteenth century. The sanctuary was given mural decorations by Clayton & Bell in 1868, and this was successfully completed in subsequent years by the incumbent, the Rev W. Wiggin. Not to everyone's taste, but a bold attempt to recreate a medieval atmosphere. It should now be preserved. The carved Norman capitals representing doves drinking from a bowl, and neck to neck, are delightful and unusual.

Hanham Abbots (8). The church is attached to the east wing of Hanham Court. The third building in this good group is a fifteenth-century tithe barn. Another barn a quarter of a mile away is called Sally-on-the-Barn because of a stone statue of Ceres standing on top of it. At Hanham Mills there is a Georgian house on the banks of the Avon, dated 1726. Christ Church, Hanham, was built in 1842 for the Rev H. T. Ellacombe by Thomas Foster, a preaching church with pews in the centre of the nave. Wesley and Whitefield preached at Hanham Mount Cottages.

Hardwicke (6). The church has interesting features, stiff-leaf capitals to the south doorway, a broad chancel and chapel with fine tomb-chests, particularly one with bold Renaissance decoration and effigies. Hardwicke Court was rebuilt in 1818 by Sir Robert Smirke. The straight canal part of a late seventeenth-century Dutch garden survives. There is a large collection of agricultural bygones, mostly housed in the building behind the house.

Harescombe (6). On the edge of the Cotswold escarpment, the charming little church has a thirteenth-century bellcote with small pinnacles, and spire, and a Transitional font with clustered shafts, both beautiful. There is also a Jacobean pulpit and a nice country Baroque monument *c.* 1726;

HIGHNAM church

in the churchyard, a good group of table-tombs. A mile or two away is Hilles, the house Detmar Blow began building for himself in c. 1914, sailing like a ship on the crest of the escarpment.

Haresfield (6). In the Gloucester Vale below the National Trust-owned beauty spot Haresfield Beacon. Haresfield Court and church, both mostly Victorian, in a flat park setting, with good trees. Church monuments.

Harnhill (17). Small church with Norman tympanum of an archangel fighting a dragon; elm trees, an early nineteenth-century rectory and a sixteenth-century manor house.

Hartpury (3). A nice group; a church of all periods, a possibly fourteenth-century tithe barn and a farmhouse. At some distance is Hartpury House, mostly by Dawber, and a training place for agriculturalists.

Haselton (14). A stone village in good sheep-walk country. Norman church.

Hasfield (3). The architect Thomas Fulljames (1811–71) buried in the churchyard. He rebuilt the north aisle of the medieval church. Hasfield Court belonged to the ancient family of Pauncefoote till 1598, and at least two rooms have sixteenth-century decoration and the initials of members of the family who died in 1559 and 1568; otherwise the house was mostly altered c. 1860.

Hatherop (15). Church and castle rebuilt by Henry Clutton for Lord de Mauley in the first half of the 1850s. Burges also worked on the church, particularly the French-Gothic south aisle which contains Monti's effigy of Barbara de Mauley. The model village is a decade later. Park and picturesque windings of the Coln.

Hawkesbury (9). A great church like a wrecked ship at the foot of the Cotswold cliff is handsome but horribly scraped inside. Village of Hawkesbury Upton higher up and rather bleak. Vulliamy's eye-catching tower monument to Lord Rupert Somerset, 1846.

Hawling (14). A high Cotswold place. Small Georgian church which escaped the notice of nineteenth-century

ecclesiologists. North wing of next-door manor in same style. Hidden in Roel Farmhouse are the remains of a church which, maybe, once served an extinct medieval village.

Hempsted (3). Fifteenth-century Perpendicular church. Lysons family monuments; their house demolished.

Hewelsfield (5). Open small field country between two stretches of the Forest of Dean. There is one of the ancient Forest churches which are set round its edge; Norman, on the north the nave roof continues over the narrow aisle to within a few feet of the ground. The road down to the Wye crosses into Monmouthshire over a graceful bridge at Brockweir, near Tintern Abbey.

Hidcote (12). Gardens made by Lawrence Johnston, now National Trust (see p. 41).

Highnam (3). Cromwellian house near Gloucester with additions by Vulliamy. Original rooms decorated with later Rococo modelled plaster work. The church built by Thomas Gambier-Parry, who himself painted the Italianate frescoes, is by Woodyer and has a tall spire, 1849–51; generally "the fulfilment of the Pugin ideal". Vicarage, school and lodge are also by Woodyer. Set in a park, with a splendid garden planted with specimen trees, and an enormous rock garden.

Hill (5). Riverside elm country; house and church in a small park, the former a very modest Victorian rebuilding, but retaining a grand seventeenth-century chimneypiece, the latter eighteenth century in atmosphere (1759).

Hillsley (6). Church 1851 by an amateur clerical architect and remarkably successful.

Hinton (5). Includes Purton and Sharpness. A good stretch of the Canal with one of Mylne's Neo-Greek bridgemen's houses with Doric columns in antis, just opposite Purton church, and Telford's lock at Sharpness, 1827. Docks dominated by new grain silo.

Horsley (6). Church rebuilt, except the Perpendicular tower, by Rickman, 1838–9. Situated on the edge of the high Beaufort country and the old cloth mills of Nailsworth. Chavenage,

between here and Tetbury, is a beautiful large sixteenth-century, or earlier, manor house.

Horton (9). Horton Court has a Norman wing alongside the Perpendicular church, and in the garden a late Gothic ambulatory.

Huntley (2). Most elaborate and original church by S. S. Teulon with naturalistic carvings by Earp, 1863. Manor house also by Teulon, very spiky like the coniferous trees round about.

Icomb (15). Early English chancel and other details. Monument of a knight, died 1431. Icomb Place, probably built for the said knight, has a great hall.

Iron Acton (8). Dark sandstone church with sculptured torso of a knight on the tower; mostly Perpendicular, restored by T. G. Jackson, with furnishings of the 1930s by F. C. Eden. Monuments, and early fifteenth-century memorial cross in churchyard. *Iron Acton Court.* An unrestored and somewhat neglected sixteenth-century house, with a large courtyard entered by a four-centred archway with mixed Gothic and Renaissance enrichments.

Kemble (17). Still a railway station, though no longer a junction; Brunel's bridges up and down the line. Church, mostly rebuilt, retains details of archaeological interest particularly the Ewen chapel.

Kempley (2). St Mary's church has wall paintings which are unique, for the chancel retains an almost complete scheme of early twelfth-century frescoes. The Norman south doorway has capitals and tympanum similar to those at Dymock. St Edward's church is by Randall Wells, 1903, built in the style of the Arts and Crafts Movement, with furnishings from Gimson's workshops at Sapperton.

Kempsford (18). The castle once belonged to Blanche, who married John of Gaunt in 1359, and who was the patroness of Chaucer; but it has long since disappeared leaving only

Iron Acton Court IRON ACTON

the fine church with its splendid Perpendicular central tower, restored by Street who added the south chancel chapel in 1858, and designed the choir-stalls with their charming finials of fanned leaves.

Kingscote (6). Thirteenth-century church, with picturesque Perpendicular tower, much restored and refenestrated by Teulon in 1851. Monuments of the Kingscote family both inside the church and in the churchyard, including an eighteenth-century triangular pyramid.

King's Stanley (6). Stanley Mills, *c*. 1812, the largest and grandest Georgian cloth mill in the Stroud

valley; five storeys, Venetian windows, and cast-iron interior construction, said to be the first fireproof building in Europe. The nearby house belonged to the mill owners and dates from much earlier times. Church medieval, restored by Bodley in 1876. Eighteenth-century tablets inside, and flat gravestones with copper plaques in the churchyard, one of which is inscribed to Ann Collins, a bar-maid, died 1804, "'Twas as she tript from cask to cask
In at a bung hole quickly fell,
Suffocation was her task
She had not time to say farewell."

Kingswood (near Wotton-under-Edge) (6). Gate-house of Kingswood Abbey survives, otherwise destroyed

at the Reformation; but this building had only just been finished. The church was built in 1723 but it has been altered and spoiled. The former rectory is an imposing mid-eighteenth-century house in the village.

Kingswood (near Bristol) (8). Old Non-conformist chapels; Whitefield's first Tabernacle in Park Road and a classical Wesleyan Chapel in Blackhorse Road. The parish church is a preaching church too; 1820 by James Foster.

Lancaut (4). Ruined church at the side of cliff cut by the Wye.

Lechlade (18). A pleasant place on the upper Thames; boating activity. The church spire looks well across a flat water meadow from St John's Bridge, the Berkshire entrance into Gloucestershire. Just down-stream is William Morris's Kelmscott, and upstream the unspoiled Wiltshire church of Inglesham. Lechlade had an enterprising late Georgian architect-builder called Pace who designed several houses such as the old vicarage, but its most delightful feature is the gazebo, a fashion repeated at the end of every respectable garden. A good example is in the garden of Church House, bordering on the churchyard which was celebrated by Shelley in "Stanzas in Lechlade churchyard", 1815. The church was rebuilt in 1473 onwards and is therefore entirely Perpendicular.

Leckhampton (14). Provided the quarry from which Regency Cheltenham was built, now a spectacular cliff climbed by generations of geological students. Church fourteenth century, with central tower and spire and vaulted sanctuary. Monument with fourteenth-century effigies of a fierce Giffard knight and his lady. Leckhampton Court also partly fourteenth century.

Leigh (13). Good Perpendicular tower to the church in flat riverside country.

Leighterton (16). Eighteenth-century farmhouses and barns; over-restored church.

Leonard Stanley (6). A splendid monastic church founded in the

St Edward's KEMPLEY
by Randall Wells, 1903

The Thames at <small>LECHLADE</small>

1120s. Note specially the lively carved Norman capitals in the chancel. Eccentric delights comprise an early sixteenth-century clock left behind by the prior, a sanctuary by Bodley, and the grave of Sir Billy Butlin's grandfather, a former vicar. The priory site is immediately to the south and the farm buildings include an eleventh-century church. The house has a front elevation added *c*. 1740. Some old houses survive in the village.

Little Dean (2). The best churchyard

in the Forest, and one of the best in the county for interesting and original gravestones. The church too is the nicest medieval church hereabouts; a vestment is preserved consisting of a pair of tunicles sewn together to make a pall or altar cloth, *c*. 1500. The gaol is one of Sir Onesiphorus Paul's four model gaols built in Gloucestershire in 1791.

Little Rissington (15). Situated on rising ground above the Dikler. Pretty village, and a partly Norman church set aside across a small ravine.

Little Sodbury (9). Manor house notable for its medieval remains including a late fifteenth-century hall, and for the fact that William Tyndale tutored the owner's sons in 1522–3.

Littleton-upon Severn (5). Partly fourteenth-century church; tiles from Thornbury Castle.

Longborough (12). The finest part of the church is the early fourteenth-century south transept with a large reticulated window and pretty dia-

<small>LEONARD STANLEY</small>

NEWNHAM from ARLINGHAM Warth

gonal buttresses. On the north the completely sealed off private pew for Sezincote, approached only by an outside entrance, was designed by C. R. Cockerell, 1822–3. Monument to Sir William Leigh, 1631, with a Renaissance canopy and effigies. Large Georgian house called Banks Fee, set in a park.

Longhope (2). Just north of it is May Hill crowned by a clump of trees to celebrate Queen Victoria's Jubilee. Church thirteenth century but much restored.

Long Newnton (16). Mostly rebuilt church *c.* 1870 by T. H. Wyatt. Monuments include ledger stones and tablets to the Estcourt family, formerly of Estcourt Park, now demolished. Priory house rebuilt by Oliver Hill, 1964.

Longney (13). Interesting church with lovely Perpendicular south porch, and timber-framed north porch. Tablets by J. Pearce of Frampton, weeping willows.

At NAILSWORTH

Lower Lemington (12). Near Todenham. Delightful small Norman church, scraped.

Lower Slaughter (15). Picturesque village on the banks of a broad and shallow brook. Nineteenth-century brick-built corn mill at one end, Benjamin Ferrey's church of 1867 at the other, with a spire now topped in fibre-glass. The manor house was built in an advanced style for these parts in 1640.

Lydbrook (2). Developed part of Dean, old housing straggling up and down the hill-sides, and not much infilling yet. Church by Woodyer, 1851.

Lydney (5). Quite a little town, but is there a hint of stagnation? The large church has a spire, a feature of the Severn-side landscape. Roman remains in the park.

Lypiatt, *see* Bisley.

Maisemore (3). Bridge rebuilt in 1956. Pretty old cottages.

Mangotsfield (8). Restored Pennant stone church with some old bits such as a nice thirteenth-century south doorway.

Marshfield (9). A village with a towny High Street composed almost entirely of Georgian or earlier houses, and including several inns; architectural merit beyond the ordinary, owing no doubt to its nearness to Bath. Church mostly Perpendicular, next to manor farm group including a medieval barn.

Matson (13). Now part of Gloucester, with large new housing estates coming almost up to the door of Matson House whence Charles I laid siege to the city.

Meysey Hampton (17). A beautiful early fourteenth-century chancel with decorated features added to an earlier building; monuments include a Baroque countrified piece with busts, early seventeenth century.

Mickleton (12). Church of all periods. Twelfth-century rood sculpture. Good selection of tablets and hatchments. Medford House is the textbook example of the transition from Tudor to Queen Anne.

Minchinhampton (16). The church has many interesting features: a beautiful south transept of the early fourteenth century, with a big window, and stone vaulted roof with

95

Manticore: a medieval, human-headed guard dog on the outer wall of the church, NORTH CERNEY

extraordinarily deep ribs, buttressed on the outside; truncated spire with a pretty sixteenth-century coronet; monuments and brasses; chancel window tracery and rere-arches by William Burges; nave stained glass by Herbert Bryans; chancel roof decorations and screen by F. C. Eden. The village is compact, owing its existence to the wool and cloth trades; there are now many outlying houses as well, a popular district. The most splendid of the eighteenth-century houses is Gatcombe Park, enlarged by Basevi. Lammas Park is crossed by sunken right of way; medieval coffin lids found.

Minsterworth (3). A rather charming and not particularly extravagant church by Henry Woodyer, set hard by the River Severn.

Miserden (13). Wooded valleys. Late Saxon church in origin; contains outstanding seventeenth-century monuments. Miserden Park Elizabethan, Victorian, enlarged by Lutyens. Hazle House, set very well and has stone griffins on its parapet. The Camp is a hamlet with a good group of old houses; but the Whiteway Colony was founded in 1898 by people who tried to live a self-supporting life, and built their own houses.

Mitcheldean (2). One of the largest churches in the Forest of Dean with a very tall spire, a nave and three aisles, and an enormous reredos with life-sized white marble figures; more interesting is the Doom painting over the screen, so sophisticated it could be a court painting, and the splendid east window by John Hayward, 1970. Much new housing.

Moreton-in-Marsh (12). A plain stone place which manages to look pretty because of its broad tree-planted main street and its central market hall (designed by Sir Ernest George in 1887).

Moreton Valance (6). A good church, Norman—sculptured tympanum, archangel fighting dragon—and Perpendicular.

Nailsworth (6 & 16). Ancient wool-town with steep and narrow streets, a quantity of elegant Jacobean and Georgian houses, several former cloth mills, Nonconformist chapels and a seventeenth-century Friends' Meeting House.

Naunton (14). A high place on the Windrush with a church largely rebuilt in the sixteenth century, but retaining its carved stone Perpendicular pulpit. Dovecote. Wild flowers.

Newent (2). Formerly a mostly brick-built Georgian town—now with much new housing—in the centre of a deeply rural district north-west of the Severn. The church is interesting in that the nave was rebuilt in 1679 and was re-orientated away from the altar and towards

NORTH CERNEY churchyard

the pulpit which was placed against the north wall. This has now been undone, but it explains some existing anomalies. The top of the fourteenth-century spire has been taken down and will be rebuilt.

Newington Bagpath (16). Simple ancient church, almost without architectural features, except for the chancel added by Teulon.

Newland (4). A fascinating church beautifully situated in hilly country on the edge of the Forest of Dean. Dates from the early thirteenth century, with later chapels, and a graceful Decorated and Perpendicular tower with pierced parapet and pinnacles. Monuments; unique effigy of a Forester of Fee in hunting costume of 1457, and a small brass of a miner of the Forest with hod and pick in hand and a candlestick in his mouth.

Newnham-on-Severn (5). Set right on the edge of the Severn, which is very broad here. Main street rises sharply to the rebuilt church, with mostly Georgian houses either side, some with ancient rope-walks going down to the river.

North Cerney (14). Mostly a twelfth-century church; note the stone sculptured corbels supporting the Perpendicular nave roof. Georgian gallery approached only by an outside stair, carved stone pulpit *c.* 1480, medieval glass, and the furnishings given by the late William Iveson Croome (such as the roodscreen and glass by his friend F. C. Eden), the late fifteenth-century French Virgin, and the fourteenth-century French Gothic processional cross; a delight for ecclesiologist and layman alike. Rectory built in 1694 and North Cerney House *c.* 1780.

Northleach (14). A wool-town and church second only to Chipping Campden and Cirencester. Church entirely rebuilt in the fifteenth century; south porch retains several images, the nave has lofty arcades with concave mouldings characteristic of the period and district. Furnishings re-arranged to fit modern liturgical use, and an east window quite unworthy of so splendid a church. The town is less spectacular but without serious blemish in spite of much new housing.

North Nibley (5). Church Perpendicular with a beautiful chancel designed by J. L. Pearson in 1861, so far unspoiled. Nibley House has a good early Georgian front. The landscape is dominated by the Tyndale Monument, a tapering stone tower erected in 1866 to the design of S. S. Teulon, in memory of the translator of the New Testament.

Norton (13). A typical brick riverside place made special by Wainlode Hill, which rises out of the Severn side to 250 feet and gives good views of the best of the Over-Severn country. Isolated church with Early English chancel, Decorated nave, and Perpendicular tower.

Notgrove (14). Norman church, with blank east wall hung with a tapestry completed in 1954, and showing the form of the fourteenth-century reredos behind. Monuments to Dick Whittington's kin with effigies. Model estate village.

Nympsfield (16). Attractive high-up place with a simple church by S. S. Teulon, 1861–63, suitably designed for the country, and added to a Perpendicular tower. The little RC church is by Charles Hansom. Both Court Farm and Street Farm must be older than their early seventeenth-century datestones.

Oakridge (16). Church 1837, gaily restored. Tradition of arts and crafts in the neighbourhood.

Oddington (15). The old church is full of interest as it is comparatively unrestored, a new church having been built in 1852, and contains wall-paintings and a Jacobean pulpit. Oddington House is attractive; it was re-modelled in Regency times.

Oldbury-upon-Severn (5). Nuclear power station; looks like a fairy castle from across the water.

NORTHLEACH

Olveston (8). Originally Norman with central tower, now a largely fourteenth-century church with a seventeenth-century chancel restored in 1841. Monuments include many tablets by Bath and Bristol sculptors.

Owlpen (16). The manor house (well-known to admirers of F. L. Griggs' etchings), barn, mill and church, make an outstanding group set about with clipped yew trees in a pretty valley near Uley.

Oxenhall (2). Typical John Middleton church of the 1860s, with a medieval tower, and one of Gloucestershire's six Norman lead fonts.

Oxenton (11). Almost unspoiled medieval church with wall-paintings and a very pretty tower.

Ozleworth (16). Norman church with central irregular hexagonal tower and other rare features, set in a circular churchyard and next a fine Georgian house, with splendid views. Newark Park is sixteenth century altered by James Wyatt in Adam style inside, and Gothic outside.

Painswick (13). Situated more than half way down a spur of land descending from Painswick Beacon to Stroud; delightful views over to Bulls Cross. Either a small town or a large village, it is architecturally a gem, with narrow streets lined by grey stone houses, gabled seventeenth century or prim Georgian.

The splendid churchyard has ninety-nine yews and an uncounted number of table-tombs, Baroque, Rococo or Renaissance. Painswick House in its park on the north, dates from 1730, with wings added by Basevi a hundred years later. This is the best; but it is true to say the place is surrounded thanks to the clothing industry by beautiful houses scattered on all sides for several miles.

Pauntley (2 & 3). S. of Redmarley. Norman church with fine south doorway, and chancel arch. Said to be the birthplace of Dick Whittington.

Pitchcombe (6). Churchyard which has several good table-tombs by Painswick masons, and Pitchcombe House a charming unaltered house of c. 1740, are the best things in this small place.

Poole Keynes (17). Simple little eighteenth-century church with a Gothic window in the tower dated 1775; other windows mid-nineteenth century. Georgian font and chandelier.

Poulton (17). Church and school by William Butterfield, 1873; but no polychrome brickwork here, where all is suitably in stone. Small square late seventeenth - century manor house.

Prestbury (14). Near Cheltenham Race-course, now joined to the town by new housing; always a favoured place to live, at the foot of Cleeve Hill the highest point in the Cotswolds. The High Street looks like part of a Cheltenham terrace on one side, and on the other is a pub with an inscription which states that Fred Archer, the jockey who "trained on toast, Cheltenham water and coffee, lived at this Prestbury inn". Church restored by Street in 1864, the same year the cemetery chapels were built by the local architect W. H. Knight.

Preston (near Cirencester) (17). A fourteenth-century bellcote distinguishes the church, of two tiers, and space for three bells.

Preston (near Dymock) (2). Norman church, and timber-framed house of *c.* 1600.

Prinknash, *see* Upton St. Leonards.

Pucklechurch (8). Church generally thirteenth century. Monuments include fourteenth-century effigies by a Bristol sculptor. Seventeenth-century houses, and new developments both industrial and residential.

Quedgeley (13). Perfectly picturesque church complete with fourteenth-century broach spire, restored by that excellent architect Woodyer, 1856, and later enlarged by his patron's architect son, Sidney Gambier Parry. Some ancient timber-framed houses, and one of Mylne's Doric canal houses at Red Bridge.

Quenington (18). The Coln meanders past the gardens of the village houses with former mills at either end. Gatehouse and dovecote survive from a preceptory of the Knights Hospitallers, and the church has two fantastic Norman doorways with tympana representing the Coronation of the Virgin and the Harrowing of Hell.

Randwick (6). Humphreys End and More Hall have Elizabethan features; higher up on a steep hill the nineteenth-century church retains a Perpendicular tower.

OWLPEN

Rangeworthy (8). Norman church with five windows by Comper, next a seventeenth-century manor house, in flat rather dull country.

Redbrook (4). On the pretty bank of the Wye. Church by J. P. Seddon with a nice window by Walter Tower.

Redmarley D'Abitot (3). Timber-framed cottages near a mostly Victorian church. The former rectory is pleasant Queen Anne with a Georgian enlargement. All now conveniently near the motorway.

Rendcomb (14). Mansion built by P. C. Hardwick in 1863 in Italianate style, now a boys' college. Square with a somewhat unrelated tower; but the stables are better and French-looking. Hardwick also built six blocks of unattractive semi-detached cottages. The church is late Perpendicular and preserves its screen, a

ODDINGTON

rare feature in Gloucestershire, and also some of its early sixteenth-century stained glass which has Renaissance motifs. Exceptionally fine Norman font with twelve arcades and figures of the Apostles.

Rodborough (6). A cattle-gridded common high up between the valleys of Stroud, with good views over the town, and dominated by Rodborough Fort, a battlemented house of *c.* 1870.

Rodmarton (16). Large manor house, building 1909 to 1926, designed by Ernest Barnsley. Church, thirteenth and fourteenth century; pretty spire.

Ruardean (2). Set in high part of Dean with spectacular views over Herefordshire. One of the series of medieval churches round the Forest fringe and with a tympanum of un-

101

PAINSWICK churchyard

usual quality belonging to the Herefordshire school of sculpture, 1130–60, as at Brinsop.

Rudford (3). Norman church with a two-bay quadripartite stone vault in the chancel.

St Briavels (4). Castle gatehouse, late thirteenth century, constructed so that it could be defended from both sides like some of the great castles in North Wales; but it has no military history, and is nothing to do with the defence of the Border. The Hall range of *c*. 1200, now used as a Youth Hostel, contains a thirteenth-century fireplace, with a chimney crowned by the horn of the Constable of the Forest. The castle was, in fact, often used as a prison. The church, alongside, is Norman

with an original south arcade and clerestory.

Saintbury (11). On the edge of the north Cotswold escarpment, a pretty village struggles down hill below the medieval church which is cruciform and has a tower with a broach spire. Inside is a wrought iron chandelier by C. R. Ashbee, 1911, besides other work by the Campden Guild of Handicraft, including the wagon roofs with their gilded bosses (before 1908), the north door with carved St Nicholas, the altar ornaments, and north chapel screen. The lead down pipes were stolen, but the rain-water heads survive. Lighting by oil lamps.

Salperton (14). Rolling Cotswold

country, park, house and tiny Norman church.

Sandhurst (3). Flat place near Gloucester with ancient scattered timber-framed farms and cottages. Rebuilt church contains one of the six late twelfth-century Gloucestershire lead fonts, and a splendid Second World War window by H. Stammers. Wallsworth Hall, though altered, is still remarkable for its original eighteenth-century architecture, 1772.

Sapperton (17). On the edge of Earl Bathurst's park, and the deep wooded valley of the river Frome; a more beautiful situation could hardly

Daneway, SAPPERTON

102

SEZINCOTE

be imagined. it was chosen by Ernest Gimson and the brothers Barnsley for their home in 1900, where they could indulge their particular brands of the Arts and Crafts Movement. Church mostly Queen Anne contains bench-ends with Jacobean caryatids and a panelled gallery. Monuments; two works by Guildo of Hereford; a canopied Renaissance tomb with effigies *c.* 1616; and the reclining figure of Sir Robert Atkyns, 1711, be-wigged and with perhaps the County History in his hand. Sapperton canal Tunnel, joining Thames and Severn, used between 1789 and 1911; is marked by carefully tree-planted mounds of extracted soil, and architectural entrances. Daneway House is earlier than 1300 and has a hall and former oratory; the high gabled building seen in our photograph was added *c.* 1620. It has a single room on each floor, with a modelled plaster ceiling, reached by a spiral staircase.

Selsey (16). Church dramatically set on the side of a steep hill by Bodley, 1862, in his French Gothic style with complete set of earliest Morris glass windows; Burne-Jones, Philip Webb, Rossetti and Ford Madox Brown.

Sevenhampton (14). Church has Perpendicular features due to the benefactions of a wool merchant who died in 1497, and has a brass here.

Sezincote (12). Famous house built in Indian style *c.* 1803–05 by S. P. Cockerell for his brother Sir Charles who had made money in the East India Company; Thomas Daniell designed the temple bridge and fountain and Repton laid out the grounds. This is the forerunner of the Brighton Pavilion.

Sharpness, see Hinton.

Sheepscombe (13). Steep wooded hills, mostly beech. Church like a china ornament.

Sherborne (15). Mansion built soon after 1551 in Renaissance style, re-built in nineteenth century in the same. Church, next door, rebuilt in Georgian times and altered again in Victorian. Monuments; a full length figure by Rysbrack, a shrouded effigy by Burman, 1661, and others by Westmacott and Bacon. Lodge Park was a "grand stand" for watching coursing, *c.* 1655, probably from designs by John Webb.

Shipton Moyne (16). Residential village in the Duke of Beaufort's country. Church mostly rebuilt, 1865, by T. H. Wyatt, but the Estcourt family chapel, 1749, survives. Monuments; fourteenth-century knights, and effigies of *c.* 1600 with Renaissance canopies.

Shipton Oliffe (14). Outstanding thirteenth-century bellcote on west gable of church.

Shipton Sollars (14). Church beautifully restored by Ellery Anderson in 1929; glass by Geoffrey Webb.

Shorncote (17). W. of South Cerney.

Delightful little church with a splendid fourteenth-century double bell-cote, and an Easter sepulchre, and a small screen in the chancel arch. Rural setting in upper Thames valley. Gravel pits.

Shurdington (13). Early fourteenth-century spire in flat over-populated country near Cheltenham.

Siddington (17). The Norman church has a south doorway with beak-heads and tympanum, and a tall cylindrical font perhaps intended for adult baptism. Perpendicular north aisle. Good group with farm buildings (an indoor riding school). Roberts House, seventeenth century, historical Quaker associations.

Siston (8). Another of Gloucestershire's lead fonts in the church. Large Elizabethan house with lodges by Sanderson Miller.

Slad (13). Slides into Stroud down a pretty valley, now made familiar by Laurie Lee's *Cider with Rosie*.

Slimbridge (5). Severn Wild Fowl

Trust preserves the flat marsh land between canal and river. Splendid thirteenth-century architecture in the church.

Snowshill (11). The manor belongs to the National Trust and has a magpie collection of musical instruments, clocks, toys, bicycles, and by-gones; presented in the period of collection, which means showing Japanese armour in the best bedroom. Open to the public April to October.

Sodbury (9). Chipping Sodbury is built either side of a broad street on an incline, with Georgian and earlier houses set well back. Church restored by G. E. Street. Old Sodbury church is Transitional; monuments include a late fourteenth-century wooden effigy of a Knight. Lyegrove House has a good garden, made since 1927.

Somerford Keynes (17). There is a Saxon north doorway to the church, on land granted to St Aldhelm in 685. Eighteenth-century Gothic survival tower. Other features of interest are the fifteenth-century screen,

which has quatrefoil openings in its bottom section as do the screens in Cirencester church, and a monument of 1645 with an effigy of a gentleman reclining on his elbow, in full dress and wig. The village is compact and is situated in the flat upper Thames valley; now almost surrounded by valuable gravel pits.

Southam (14). Near Prestbury. Becoming a residential area near Cheltenham, with a great many new houses built in reconstructed stone. Situated at the foot of Cleeve Hill, the highest point of the Cotswold escarpment, Southam Delabere is one of the largest Elizabethan houses in the county, with plenty of features remaining from that period; but enlarged by Lord Ellenborough, Governor-General of India 1841–44, with a Neo-Norman keep and Gothic tower to accommodate his servants. A curious summer-house commemorates his staff in India, and he also rebuilt the little church, and filled it with fabulous objects.

South Cerney (17). Large village on the edge of the gravel pits, and

SHARPNESS, 20,000 ton grain silo.

S T A N W A Y House: The Gatehouse

upper Thames; bridges, gazebos, manor houses and a street called Bow-wow. Interesting Norman and Decorated church; doorway with beak-heads, window with ballflower. Wooden head of Christ from twelfth-century rood, a work of great intensity.

Southrop (18). Of all the unlikely places this is where Keble sowed the first seeds of the Oxford Movement. Stone built village with pretty manor and mill. The font in the church is famous for its virtuous armoured women trampling on vice.

Standish (6). Important chest-hospital in grounds of former Standish House, once a hunting lodge to enable Lord Sherborne to go with the Berkeley. Church outstanding; all one period, early fourteenth

century, and houses the re-furbished monument of Sir Winston Churchill's ancestor. Also the ledger stone of Bishop Frampton; Pepys thought he preached "most like an apostle . . . it was much the best time that I ever spent in church".

Stanley Pontlarge (14). Church Norman and Neo-Norman, in remote situation.

Stanton (11). Perfectly preserved village without blemish. This is partly due to the sympathetic restorations of its former owner, architect Sir Philip Stott, who lived here 1906–37. His good example has been followed by the Rural District Council whose council houses are here built in traditional style and local material. The ancient church is distinguished by the twentieth-century furnishings and glass of Sir Ninian Comper.

Stanway (11). Stanton's aristocratic neighbour, a delightful group of golden buildings, medieval church and tithe barn, Tudor mansion, and the Jacobean gatehouse, most memorable of them all with its curvilinear gables surmounted by scallop shells. High up in the gardens on the east side is a Pyramid, from which in the eighteenth century came a formal waterfall and canal. Splendid specimen trees are planted hereabouts. The war memorial has a bronze St George by Alexander Fisher, and names by Eric Gill. Memorial hall is Neo-Classical by Detmar Blow. In the famous days of country-house cricket and political hostesses Sir James Barrie designed a cricket pavilion for the Countess of Wemyss.

Staunton (By Monmouth) (1). One of the nicest of the old churches on the edge of the Forest of Dean. In the churchyard is the grave of David Mushet, the metallurgist whose experiments at nearby Coleford were to completely change the steel industry.

Staunton (By Newent) (3). Chartist houses of 1847 at Snig's End and Lowbands. Church mostly ancient with an unusual arcade with straight sided arches and lozenge-shaped piers, and a small chapel with a charming little wooden roof, and amusing monument to a long-nosed Elizabethan family.

Staverton (13). Aerodrome for the Dowty works. The centre of the ancient village is its church which still preserves an atmosphere of

peace and quiet. It has a massive tower on the south, the top stage of which must have been taken down before 1712, judging from the datestone on the parapet.

Stinchcombe (5). Church largely rebuilt by J. L. Pearson in 1855. Tractarian influence; Isaac Williams was vicar and the Rev. Sir George Prevost squire, both former curates of the Kebles. Several large houses on the escarpment edge, and tremendous views over the Severn plane. Stancombe Park has a very late attempt at a romantic garden which does not quite come off.

Stoke Gifford (8). Stoke Park was

once a great stately home near Bristol, built by the Berkeleys in the sixteenth century on an artificial terrace which survives. It was rebuilt by Lord Botetourt, *c.* 1760, before he became Governor of Virginia, with rooms decorated by the best Bristol stuccoists and grounds laid out by Thomas Wright, hot from Badminton and no doubt recommended by his lordship's sister who was now Duchess of Beaufort. In the church the Duchess had a room with a fireplace on the north of the sanctuary. It is now the vestry; the mansion is a hospital.

Stoke Orchard (13). Small church with wall-paintings comprising the cycle of the life of St James of

TETBURY Market House

TETBURY

Compostela. Bristol was most probably where pilgrims sailed from, when going to Compostela.

Stonehouse (13). On the edge of the industrial belt of the Stroud Valley. Nineteenth-century mills and modern factories, old traditional houses mixed with Victorian brick. Stonehouse Court is Elizabethan, restored and altered by Lutyens. Wycliffe College was founded in 1882.

Stow-on-the-Wold (15). Large open square or market place, surrounded by picturesque stone-built houses, many selling antiques, is tourist attraction. Church central, of all periods and interesting; Wailes' most violent colours in the windows. Post-Second World War housing of stone represents a seldom-achieved ideal.

Stowell (14). Great estate with many acres of park, farmland, and woods. Elizabethan mansion enlarged by Sir John Belcher in the 1890s, and tiny late twelfth-century cruciform church containing Doom wall-painting.

Stroud (13). The centre of early industrial development with mills spread out along the river Frome,

processing either the raw wool or the finished cloth, or both. Stroudwater scarlets and blues for military uniforms became famous. By 1824 the Frome and its tributaries worked 150 mills. Canals brought coal from the midlands in the later era of steam-power; but the district was hit by the depressions of the 1830s and 1870s, from which it never recovered. Some six cloth-mills remain still producing the finest quality. Other mills have passed their original usefulness, and the tall buildings are redundant. The town is built on extremely steep hills with narrow streets; few clothiers' houses survive and the more interesting old houses are to be found on the outskirts. There is, however, a fine public building, the Stroud Subscription Rooms, built in 1833, which has a splendid classical front. Next door is a good Congregational chapel, both by Charles Baker of Painswick; but their surroundings lack the dignity they deserve. The best of the churches is Temple Moore's All Saints, Uplands, 1908–10; but the parish church of St Lawrence is not without interest and contains a reredos by G. G. Scott (junior), stained glass by Bewsey, and interesting monuments. There is an excellent Museum.

Sudeley Castle (14). Romantic buildings in beautiful setting at the foot of the Cotswold escarpment near Winchcombe. Once the property of Richard III, the ruins of whose splendid apartments can still be seen in the inner court, it was given to Henry VIII's widow and her husband Seymour in 1547. Her effigy, by J. B. Philip, lies under a canopy by Sir Gilbert Scott in the church in the gardens. The castle was slighted in the Civil War and became almost uninhabitable till it was bought and restored by the Dent family in 1837.

Swell (15). Two villages, Upper and Nether, prettily situated on the Dikler, which at the former flows through an enlarged mill pond and under an eighteenth-century bridge. The manor house here is Jacobean and the small church Norman. Nether Swell's Norman church is now only the south aisle, as a new nave and chancel were added in the nineteenth century with windows and wall-paintings by Clayton & Bell. In this parish is Abbotswood, a house designed by Lutyens, which has a well-known garden. There is

TETBURY church
by Francis Hiorn, 1776

108

also an extraordinary cottage, built evidently with pieces left over from Sezincote, at a time when distinction was desired for the exploitation of a chalybeate spring into a spa.

Swindon (13). Village, now a suburb of Cheltenham, with attractive new housing estates. The church retains its rare hexagonal Norman tower, but was otherwise insensitively messed about in 1845.

Syde (14). Small Norman church, manor, and a few farms set on the edge of a well-wooded valley.

Taynton (2). Pretty undulating country, hedge-row trees, under the shadow of May Hill and its tree-clump top. Church destroyed in civil war and rebuilt by order of Parliament in 1648; not orientated to the east. Chancel added in nineteenth century. Taynton House, with its brick barn, cider-mill, and ox-house, represents the building achievement of a successful yeoman; the barn is dated 1695 and has stone cartouches with Latin tags.

Teddington (11). Not much of a village at all but the church is full of surprises. A tower arch and west window, beautiful examples of late thirteenth-century work, were brought here from Hailes Abbey, and incorporated into the church in 1567. Other delights are the Commonwealth furnishings and texts, and the William and Mary coat of arms painted very large on the south wall.

Temple Guiting (14). Very good country at the head of the Windrush valley. The church is set on one side of a wooded ravine with Temple Guiting house on the other. Its metamorphosis is interesting; a possession of the Knights Templar, it retains Norman features with Decorated and Perpendicular additions which were again altered in Georgian and Victorian times, and on which large sums have had to be spent in restoration at the present time.

Barton, Kineton and Ford are hamlets all with delightful houses, and where good sport can be expected after a meet of the North Cotswold hounds.

Tetbury (16). A small grey town not far from Badminton, set in rolling stone country where a Cotswold spur separates upper Thames from Avon. The name of the White Hart Hotel has been changed to the Snooty Fox, perhaps rather an urban gesture though not without implication. Vulliamy's ballroom on the first floor for the Beaufort Hunt is no longer used as such. Opposite where all roads meet is a seventeenth-century Market House for weighing and selling wool, when Tetbury was an important wool-market, one of the nearest to the Stroudwater mills. There are lots of elegant houses both seventeenth century and Georgian, standing cheek by jowl in Long Street in impressive array. The environs of the Georgian Gothic church are green and close, an attractive setting for such pretty pioneering architecture. Samuel Saunders, one of the gentlemen who commissioned Francis Hiorn to build it in 1776, is commemorated thus:

> In a vault underneath
> lie several of the Saunderses,
> late of this parish: particulars
> the Last Day will disclose.

The family, who seem from this to have been both proud, humble and defiant, lived at The Grove at Tetbury Upton where there is another splendid house of Bristol type built in 1752; both have small parks.

Tewkesbury (10). The description of a peaceful town, by Anthony West in the *Shell Guide* of 1939, cannot be upheld, with traffic coming off the motorway and roaring through the main street; but a change no doubt will come when the by-pass is built. The site of the town was so confined by the rivers that any expansion after the later Middle Ages was impossible. Any increase that was required in the number of houses was achieved by raising the density of building, and particularly by building in the alleys behind the main streets. This characteristic feature was caused by the increase

of population owing to the change from the cloth industry in which most of the work was done in the master's house, to that of knitting carried on in the homes of the workers. There was hardly any new building between the 1850s and the 1930s. Most of the houses are very much older indeed. The cottages in Church Street are pre-Reformation and possibly represent one of the earliest examples of uniform medieval town development, built by the Abbey and let to the townsfolk as a speculative development. They are timber-framed like most of the houses in the town though many others have Georgian brick fronts.

The descent of the lordship of Tewkesbury is historical and romantic. Granted by William the Conqueror to his Queen Matilda it came to William Rufus's cousin Robert FitzHamon, who founded the Abbey and died in 1107 before its consecration in 1121. FitzHamon's daughter married Robert FitzRoy, natural son of Henry I. He was made Earl of Gloucester and continued the building. From the FitzRoys it passed to the de Clares who held it for nearly 200 years, then to the Despencers, all patrons of the church and buried therein. The collection of tombs, chantry chapels and monuments are second only to those in Westminster Abbey. The final disaster came in 1471 when the Battle of Tewkesbury was joined on the morning of May 4, ending in the crushing defeat of the Lancastrians who were driven to take refuge in the Abbey hotly pursued by the Yorkist brothers Edward IV, Richard of Gloucester and George of Clarence. The Duchess of Clarence was sister to the Princess of Wales and they were co-heiresses of the lordship of Tewkesbury; but the poor little Lancastrian Prince of Wales was killed without mercy. The Despencer family are portrayed in the windows of the Abbey presbytery. For a detailed description of the Abbey the reader is recommended to look at Vol. 11 of *Gloucestershire* in the "Buildings of England", Penguin Books.

Uley (6). Hetty Pegler's Tump is a Neolithic long barrow where some twenty-eight people were buried in a still accessible roofed chamber, situated on the edge of the Cotswold escarpment above Uley. The village straggles down the hill and is packed full of houses of architectural distinction, built by the descendants of clothiers in an age of elegance. Broadcloth was made here and also Spanish cloth, and Uley blues were almost as famous as Stroudwater reds. The church by S. S. Teulon is as eccentric and novel as any member of the Victorian Society could hope for; the Nonconformist chapel, charming Georgian gothic, 1790.

Upleadon (3). Excessively rural vale country, by an isolated farmhouse, the church stands rather precariously on a mound of clay and has an early Tudor half-timbered tower.

Upper Slaughter (15). Very pretty secluded Cotswold village, with an open square with cottages remodelled by Lutyens, and roads leading down to a bridge and a ford across the brook. All the houses are built of stone from the numerous old quarries and most still have tile-stone roofs. A rather mucked-about church still retains many details of beauty and interest.

Upton St Leonards (13). Becoming swallowed up in Gloucester but winding lanes and timber-framed cottages survive at Bondend, near Bowden Hall, a fine double bow-fronted house of 1770. Church much altered in the nineteenth century contains a good monument by Ricketts of Gloucester *c.* 1745. *Prinknash Abbey* was built as a grange and hunting lodge for the Abbot of St Peter's Abbey, Gloucester, and partly dates from the time of the last abbot. It was enlarged in the nineteenth century and is now once more a Benedictine monastery. There is a carved head of Henry VIII *c.* 1510. In 1774 Horace Walpole visited Prinknash and ported: "It

stands on a glorious impracticable hill, in the midst of a little forest of beech, and commanding Elysium. The chapel is low and small, but antique, and with painted glass, with many angels in their coronation robes. Under a window is a barbarous bas-relief of Harry Young." All of which is still true.

Wapley (8). Beautiful church with an elaborate tomb of 1475.

Washbourne, Great and Little (11). Two churches, both delightful; one with a font in the choir, and both retaining old furnishings.

Westbury-on-Severn (2). Westbury Court Garden, a Dutch garden created between 1696 and 1705. Some twenty houses illustrated by Kip in Atkyns's "Present State of Gloucestershire", *c.* 1712, had Dutch gardens, and this is the only one completely to escape the fashionable cult of the picturesque which fol-

115

LITTLE WASHBOURNE

lowed. After years of neglect it is now (1970) being restored by the National Trust. Church has detached tower with wooden shingle-covered spire, a landmark up and down the river.

Westcote (15). Isolated stone village overlooking the Evenlode. Much restored but carefully tended church. Home of Anglican convent.

West Dean (5). Comprises a large part of the central portion of the Forest of Dean. After disputes ceased to be heard at St Briavels Castle, a Court of Speech was set up at Speech House overlooking Cannop valley. This became the focal point of the Forest, with a Charles II court-room, which was first used in 1680 with a session of the Mine Law Court. It is now a hotel; but the court-room is still used.

At Parkend in the heart of the Forest there is a delightful church built on an octagonal plan in 1822, with most of its original fittings, and contemporary rectory. Christ Church Berry Hill is earlier, 1816, but duller, and Bream has a church rebuilt by William White in 1860.

Westerleigh (8) Good Perpendicular church tower though built of Pennant stone, an unattractive material compared with the oolitic limestone of the hills. At Coalpit Heath, Butterfield's very early church, 1844, and the vicarage which marks an influential turning point towards ascetic functionalism in nineteenth-century domestic architecture.

Westonbirt with Lasborough (6). The Westonbirt Arboretum has probably the most interesting collection of trees in Britain. The almost equally well-known girls' school is housed in a mansion by Vulliamy (1863–70) intended to resemble Elizabethan Wollaton Hall. Church at Lasborough also by Vulliamy; but not nearly so successful. Lasborough Park, castellated Tudor Gothic, by James Wyatt, 1794. Lasborough Manor, c. 1610, is sometimes open to the public; good Renaissance chimney-pieces.

Weston-Sub-Edge (11). Pretty stone village with several good houses in the main street; over-restored church.

Whaddon (3). Thirteenth-century church with Perpendicular tower, and east window by Comper.

Whelford (18). Small church by G. E. Street, 1864.

Whitminster (6 & 13). Village straddling the main Bristol road, from which a twisting lane leads to the church and Whitminster House, on the banks of the Frome. In the eighteenth century the house belonged to Richard Owen Cambridge, a minor poet whose recreations were landscape-gardening (he told Capability Brown he hoped to die first so as to see heaven before it was improved), mechanics and navigation. Riparian pleasures were here to hand, and in 1750 he entertained the Prince of Wales in a Venetian gondola. The Stroudwater Canal (now mostly disused) crosses the navigable Gloucester–Berkeley Canal, with swing bridges and Grecian keepers' houses nearby.

Whittington (14). Stone village, small and compact, a little distance from church and Whittington Court, in good country half way up the Cotswold edge. The church contains

116

monuments and the house is Tudor with Renaissance details.

Wick (8). Church completed by Butterfield in 1850. Wick Court seventeenth century, now company offices; the place is being developed.

Wickwar (8). Described in the sixteenth century by Leland as a "pretty clothing town", it remains a small town or rather a large village with a long High Street packed with Georgian stucco-fronted houses. Over-restored church set apart on a mound, with a former rectory by Devey.

Willersey (11). Village houses built either side of a long wide green, with one set back with imposing stone gate-piers in front of a duck pond. Best feature of the church, as is so often the case, is its Perpendicular tower.

Winchcombe (14). Small town with a very ancient history. Few Benedictine abbeys of such significance have so completely disappeared, but then its demolition was carried out by the Lord Seymour of Sudeley who did not believe in half-measures; there has never been any serious attempt at excavation. At least one pre-

Reformation domestic building survives, an inn for pilgrims, now called the George Hotel; on the spandrels of the doorway are carved the initials of Abbot Richard Kidderminster, who resigned in 1525. An earlier abbot built the chancel of the church *c.* 1465. The nave was the responsibility of the townspeople aided by Sir Ralph Boteler of nearby Sudeley Castle. A fine Perpendicular church is the result. Prosperity was there, from the wool trade and then from growing tobacco, and later from the paper mills. Winchcombe is proud of its history. Many of the houses tightly packed in the main street

Westonbirt Arboretum

117

have gardens going down to the river Isbourne; one has a shell grotto. A descending row of almshouses was designed by Sir Gilbert Scott, another of the many signs of bountiful patronage from Sudeley Castle. Winchcombe seems satisfied with the past and has wisely escaped development. Its air of somnolence is no doubt deceptive.

Windrush (15). Pretty village on the river of this name, with a triangular green, and houses all built of the superb local oolitic limestone; indeed the perfect condition of the church very much impressed the Royal Commission who were choosing stone for the new Houses of Parliament in 1830. Norman, with a double row of beaked heads round the doorway, and the churchyard has a splendid group of Baroque table tombs.

Winson (14). Warm-coloured stone village; a small Norman church, and a dignified mid-eighteenth-century house next door. The carefully preserved Coln is a good spot for fishing when the mayfly is up.

Winstone (14). Wold village, a bit bleak, and no buildings of quality except the church which is Saxon.

Winterbourne (8). Residential place near Bristol with old church containing many fine monuments. At Winterbourne Down the church is by G. E. Street.

Withington (14). Pretty stone village with everything; a fine church, rectory, manor, dovecote, mill and even a restaurant well-known for its cuisine.

Woodchester (6). Romantic industrial scenery. Old mills, clothiers' houses. Southfield Mill House the most interesting. The Cottage Improvement Society has done much good in preserving the village (e.g. Court Cottages, Selsley Hill). Site of a large Roman villa; a mosaic pavement situated in the old churchyard is uncovered every ten years or so. New church by Teulon. Dominican priory and church by Charles Hansom, 1846; thoroughly Puginesque. Woodchester Park situated in a secluded valley about three miles long with a chain of five lakes, well-wooded and owned by a private forestry company. Unfinished house designed by Benjamin Bucknall, translator of Viollet-le-Duc, *c.* 1858. Only inhabited by birds and bats.

Woolaston (5). Characterless between Dean and Severn. Mucked-about church and large rectory.

Woolstone (11). Pretty situation. Church with leaning tower.

Wormington (11). The Grange, a late Georgian bow-fronter with Neo-Greek additions in superb ashlar. Saxon crucifix found here, now in the church; it may have come from Winchcombe Abbey.

Wotton-under-Edge (6). Created a borough in 1252; Corporation abolished 1883. Between 1617 and 1811 some twenty-six mayors were clothiers or woolmen; but with the Industrial Revolution, and the development of worsted, Wotton, like many other places in the district, closed her mills and has avoided doing anything very energetic ever since. However strains of eccentricity have appeared from time to time. Isaac Pitman, inventor of shorthand, was told that because of his religious beliefs he could expect to be "hunted out of the town like a mad dog". More Adey, fantastic bearded friend of Oscar Wilde, claimed to be Squire of Wotton, and spent much time looking for treasure in Under-the-Hill House.

The High Street, busy and unself-consciously attractive, is lined onto the police station, which satisfactorily closes the view that end. From 31 Long Street a complete room was sold to the Victoria and Albert in 1924. At the other end are seventeenth-century almshouses. Fine church, good Perpendicular tower. Organ, George I. Monuments include the Berkeley brasses, late fourteenth century.

Wyck Rissington (15). Best thirteenth-century east end of any church in the county; the incunabula of tracery.

Yanworth (14). Small Norman church in a farmyard on the edge of Stowell Park.

Yate (8). New overspill town for Bristol and Bath. Church with upstanding Perpendicular pinnacled tower. Modern shopping centre, begun 1965.

Bristol

Bristol has never been part of Gloucestershire, not anyway since 1373 when it was given county status. A Roman port existed at Sea Mills, and there was a Saxon monastery at Westbury-on-Trym; but Bristol was not a Roman city, nor was it very important in Saxon times. During the Middle Ages and later, however, Bristol became one of the most prosperous towns in England, second only to London, and with an equally busy port. It now ranks only ninth in size, and has been severely bombed, and in some cases ill-treated by unsuitable new building; but for John Betjeman and many others it is still the "most beautiful, interesting, and distinguished city in England".

It would be strange then if Bristol's influence or what is called Bristol Fashion was not to be found in Gloucestershire. In the eighteenth century that part of Gloucestershire south of a line running from Aust to Sodbury was known as the Bristol Quarter. North of this is the Vale of Berkeley. It was Robert Fitzharding, the 1st Lord Berkeley, who founded the Augustinian abbey in Bristol in 1140, now Bristol Cathedral. The architecture of the Berkeley chapel, however, is early fourteenth century, and shows affinity with the design of the "Berkeley Arch" at Berkeley Castle. To take other examples at random, think how like the top of the tower of St Stephen's church is to the coronet of Gloucester cathedral, though of course on a much smaller scale. And the joiner who made the beautiful Elizabethan Renaissance panelling in the Red Lodge, must be the same as he who did the panelling in the Old Deanery, Gloucester. In the eighteenth century Bristol's architects and craftsmen were widely influential. Before Palladianism swept all before it, the English were developing a Baroque architecture of their own. This rather naïve Baroque was a modern style compared with the

gabled houses still being built in the country. John Strahan of Bristol was one who practised in the style and is represented in Queen Charlotte Street. Possible Gloucestershire houses by him are Frampton-on-Severn Court, Tetbury Upton House, and Painswick House. The Rococo modelled plasterwork of William Stocking so perfectly exemplified at the Royal Fort with foxes chasing birds about a grape vine in high relief, can also be found in one form or another in many a Gloucestershire house as far away as The Beacon, Painswick or Higham Court near Gloucester. And surely the saucer-domes of Christ Church, Broad Street, by William Paty, are derived from Charles Evans' church at Badminton, showing that Bristolians were not above taking an idea or two from their ducal neighbour.

John Betjeman has delighted to describe Bristol in his own inimitable language. "To me the best port of all is Bristol," he says. "There is no city in England with so much character. It is a town associated with rich men in the tobacco, wine and chocolate trades." On the one hand, there is the "old city, the port on the Avon, with narrow streets, old churches, timber-framed houses and an eighteenth-century theatre", and on the other is "a second city, Clifton, like Bath, a late Georgian spa on the heights of the Avon Gorge. The Gorge is crossed by Brunel's Suspension Bridge, which is a delicate balanced structure, like an insect of enormous size pausing astride the rocks and trees". Bristol has been bombed; but its "strong character is not destroyed, nor have all its best buildings and its narrow alleyways disappeared. Bristol will never die".

Anyone who spends only a day exploring the centre of Bristol will know that this is true, though it must be admitted that change there has been. Inevitable rebuilding resulting from the

above: Clifton Suspension Bridge
below: The floating harbour and Cathedral

p. 122 St Mary Redcliffe, detail
p. 123 St Mary Redcliffe

by Sir George Oatley in 1925. Clearly we must now get rid of our car, and there are many multi-storeyed car parks so it is not an impossibility. A walk round the old town can be achieved in comfort and the rewards are greatly satisfying. If we enter through St John's Gateway in the old city wall, St John's Church (fourteenth century) is above us, and Broad Street rises in front. On the left are the Art Nouveau premises of Edward Everard faced in brightly coloured faience, and further along C. R. Cockerell's building for the Bank of England, and the Grand Hotel, 1869, with a top loggia like a Florentine palace. Finally Christ Church, another building recently cleaned, with its beautiful golden-coloured tower and spire piercing the blue sky of a summer day. In Corn Street, All Saints Church—partly Norman and the rest Perpendicular—contains the Rysbrack effigy of Edward Colston. The Old Council House, by Sir Robert Smirke, is a Greek building with Ionic columns, next the fantastically rich façade of Lloyds Bank, 1858. The Commercial Rooms, by Busby of Brighton, Neo-Greek again; opposite is the Exchange, for this is the heart of commercial life in the city, by John Wood the Elder, 1740–3. On the pavement stand the four Brass Nails, baluster-shaped pillars of sixteenth- and seventeenth-century date; hence the expression "pay on the nail". Lower down in Clare Street, the red terracotta Loire château by Waterhouse for the Prudential. St Stephen's church, built to meet the needs of a merchant community who practised the invocation of numerous saints, is all mid-fifteenth century with a Perpendicular tower given by a Mayor. King Street is now preserved with all its fine buildings, though the Robinson Building can sometimes be seen at one end to spoil the illusion. At the end nearest the docks is a tall old timber-framed pub called Llandoger Trow; then there are gabled almshouses, and the Coopers Hall with a Palladian façade by William Halfpenny. The Theatre Royal does not look anything from the outside but is in fact the oldest playhouse in England still in use. It was designed in 1766 by James Paty. The former Public Library building, by another Paty, c. 1740, classical and ashlar-faced. Finally the

Clifton Terraces:
p. 126 Windsor Terrace
p. 127 Royal York Crescent
from the Paragon

Merchant Venturers Almshouses, of which only two sides of the square survive, and these, in spite of being overpowered by enormous towering blocks of offices, still proclaim for the inhabitants that

"Freed from all storms, the tempest and the rage
Of billows, here we spend our age."

So much for the ever-changing heart of Bristol.

Across Queen Square, called so after Queen Anne and containing the marvellous equestrian

Temple church BRISTOL: the leaning tower

statue of William III by Rysbrack, lies the former district of Redcliffe now criss-crossed by motorways and fly-overs. St Mary Redcliffe, however, remains incomparable among the parish churches of England; aisled transepts, and ambulatory behind the altar, projecting lady chapel, stone vaults, tall clerestory requiring flying buttresses, spire (292 feet high) and fabulous Decorated doorway to the hexagonal north porch, so intricate and bossy that it could derive from India. This master mason was also involved in the building of the Cathedral back across Queen Square and the floating harbour.

Bristol Cathedral, like St Mary's, is built of inferior oolite. The chapter house is Norman. The period between 1298 and about 1330 was when Bristol led European architecture, and the master of Bristol rebuilt the eastern parts of the abbey church. His handling of space in the Cathedral is proof of his genius, and the chancel and the chancel-aisles are vaulted with flying ribs. The cusping of ribs also seems to have been invented here. The nave and western towers were built by G. E. Street in a rather dull but quite complimentary manner, 1868–88. Immediately to the west is Charles Holden's Municipal Library, 1906, in a style which must have been influenced by Mackintosh's Glasgow Art School. Adjacent in College Green the Council House, 1936–56, by Vincent Harris (of the Stockholm Town Hall period), has golden unicorns on the roof. The Statue of Cabot is by Sir Charles Wheeler. The Lord Mayor's Chapel was built for the Hospital of St Mark, Early English, restored by J. L. Pearson, and full of monuments. Before leaving this area, mention must be made of the old Christmas Steps, 1669. They lead up from Colston Street, are very picturesque and full of promising antique shops. St Michael's Hill and much of the character of Kingsdown

Blaise Hamlet by John Nash

Bristol country: Warmley from Siston Common

comes from its street furniture, raised pavements, railings, old lamps, steps and cobbles. Park Street and Queen's Road lead up past the University to Clifton.

Clifton. Royal York Crescent, 1810–20, is the finest of the Regency terraces, with a promenade above the stables. On the western end is The Paragon, 1809–14, a curved cul-de-sac high above the Avon Gorge; each round porch has a curved door. Fine buildings of this period are also to be seen in Cornwallis Crescent, 1791–*c.* 1830; Clifton Hill, mid-eighteenth century, including Bishop's House, 1711, Clifton Hill House, 1746–50, by Isaac Ware, and Goldney House, *c.* 1720, with alterations by Waterhouse 1860–5, Princes Buildings, *c.* 1796; Rodney Place, late eighteenth century; and Windsor Terrace, 1790–1810. Clifton College is by Charles Hansom, 1860. Beyond is Clifton Down and further to the east Redland, where Redland Chapel is a "must"; built by William Halfpenny in 1741–3, it contains the most sumptuous wood-carving by Thomas Paty. Below Clifton beside the Avon is the former Hotwells Spa, and near here the Cumberland Basin, a complex of bridges, flyovers and underpasses with the largest swing bridge in the country. Docks, Victorian warehouses and new buildings.

On the other side of the docks area *Temple Meads Station* contains Brunel's train shed, with a wooden hammerbeam roof truss. At *Brislington*, Arno's Court is Strawberry Hill Gothic, with castellated stables built of black copper slag. Arno's Vale Cemetery has Greek Doric lodges, and some very elaborate tombs. Quieter is the Convent of the Sisters of Charity in *Redcatch Road*, where Anglican nuns worship in a chapel by Bodley.

The suburbs of Bristol include Henbury, Kings Weston, Shirehampton, Stapleton, Stoke Bishop and Westbury-on-Trym. At *Henbury* are a medieval church, several Georgian houses and Blaise Castle House, 1796, by William Paty, now a museum, with an orangery by Nash, who also designed the well-known thatched cottages in their picturesque setting. *Kings Weston House* was designed by Vanbrugh, *c.* 1710, with monumental chimneys. *Shirehampton* is mostly twentieth-century estates. *Stapleton* and *Stoke Bishop* have churches by John Norton. *Westbury-on-Trym* was a very early monastic foundation. Remains of the fifteenth-century college buildings are being restored by the National Trust. In nearby Canford Cemetery is a tombstone with sculpture by Eric Gill.

129

Appendix

Abies cilicica	Cilician fir	Speech House	66 ft × 7 ft 1 in
Fastest growing and healthiest known			
Abies concolor lowiana	Low's fir	Westonbirt	125 ft × 12 ft 6 in
Abies grandis	Grand fir	Batsford	150 ft × 12 ft 8 in
		Westonbirt	145 ft × 14 ft 0 in
Araucaria araucana	Chile pine	Highnam	68 ft × 9 ft 1 in
Cedrus deodara	Deodara	Tortworth	100 ft × 13 ft 7 in
Cedrus libani	Cedar of Lebanon	Stanway	100 ft × 25 ft 4 in
A very fine bole for 10 ft, among the very biggest			
Chamaecyparis nootkatensis	Nootka cypress	Westonbirt	93 ft × 10 ft 0 in
One of the biggest in Britain			
Cupressus lusitanica stricta		Westonbirt	80 ft × 10 ft 0 in
Only specimen known in Britain			
Juniperus drupacea	Syrian juniper	Stanway	45 ft × 5 ft @3 ft
The two finest in the country		Batsford	47 ft × 5 ft 6 in @3 ft
Ginkgo biloba		Badminton	70 ft × 10 ft 0 in
		Hatherop Castle	57 ft × 5 ft 5 in
Larix occidentalis	Western larch	Tortworth	73 ft × 4 ft 10 in
Second best known			
Picea brachytyla		Westonbirt	81 ft × 5 ft 6 in
Tallest known of a rare and lovely Chinese spruce			
Picea breweriana	Brewer's spruce	Westonbirt	35 ft
Famous groups			
Picea orientalis	Caucasian spruce	Stanway	80 ft × 10 ft 6 in
One of the biggest boles			
Picea pungens glauca	Blue Colorado spruce	Batsford	71 ft × 5 ft 6 in
One of the finest in Britain—several there similar			
Pinus contorta	Shore pine	Westonbirt	58 ft × 8 ft 9 in
Big, broad tree; features in Dallimore and Jackson			
Pinus coulteri	Coulter's pine	Stanway	66 ft × 7 ft 8 in
Splendid young tree. Only two bigger—both much older			
Pinus leucodermis	Bosnian pine	Colesbourne	60 ft × 5 ft 0 in
Fine young specimen, among biggest			
Pinus peuce	Macedonian pine	Westonbirt	78 ft × 7 ft 8 in
Bigger of a fine pair			
Pinus ponderosa	Western yellow pine	Highnam	82 ft × 12 ft 8 in
One of the biggest in girth			
Pinus ponderosa	Western yellow pine	Westonbirt	105 ft × 8 ft 2 in
One of the finest shaped crowns			
Pinus strobus	Weymouth pine	Cannop (Dean)	120 ft × 11 ft 3 in
One of the tallest known			
Sequoia sempervirens	Coastal redwood	Stanway	100 ft × 15 ft 9 in
		Huntley Manor	114 ft × 16 ft 3 in
Sequoiadendron giganteum	Wellingtonia	Westonbirt	138 ft × 21 ft 3 in
Among the biggest			
Acer macrophyllum	Oregon maple	Westonbirt Park	68 ft × 9 ft 9 in
Two biggest in Britain		Westonbirt Arboretum	72 ft × 9 ft 4 in
Acer opalus	Italian maple	Tortworth	66 ft × 8 ft 11 in
Biggest known in Britain			
Acer Rubrum	Red maple	Westonbirt	75 ft × 4 ft 10 in
Tallest known in Britain			
Acer saccharinum	Silver maple	Westonbirt	100 ft × 8 ft 5 in
Tallest and biggest known		Tortworth	90 ft × 12 ft 2 in
Acer van Volxemii	Van Volxem's maple	Westonbirt	73 ft × 6 ft 8 in
Tallest and biggest known		Tortworth	53 ft × 8 ft 6 in

Aesculus turbinata	Japanese horse chestnut	Westonbirt House	55 ft × 6 ft 10 in
Oldest (1st), tallest, biggest and best in Britain respectively		Westonbirt Arboretum	70 ft × 5 ft 3 in
		Westonbirt Arboretum	52 ft × 7 ft 1 in
		Tortworth	51 ft × 6 ft 9 in
Aesculus hippocastanum	Horse chestnut	Badminton	90 ft × 16 ft 10 in
Alnus cordata	Italian alder	Westonbirt	90 ft × 8 ft 0 in
Tallest known			
Betula ermanii	Japanese birch	Westonbirt	55 ft × 7 ft 4 in
Finest known			
Carya cordiformis	Bitternut (Hickory)	Westonbirt	80 ft × 5 ft 0 in
		Tortworth	85 ft × 6 ft 2 in
Castanea sativa	Sweet chestnut	Highnam	80 ft × 33 ft 4 in
Curious stool—girthed at 1 ft 6 in. Mentioned in Elwes and Henry			
Castanea sativa	Sweet chestnut	Tortworth Churchyard	35 ft @ 1 ft
Often claimed as oldest tree in Britain—poor claim really. Very famous			
Catalpa bignonioides	Indian bean	Batsford	60 ft × 4 ft 8 in
Tallest known			
Davidia involucrata	Dove-tree	Westonbirt	57 ft × 4 ft 10 in
Fagus sylvatica	Beech	Batsford	115 ft × 12 ft 2 in
Fine big bole			
Fagus fastigiata	Dawyck beech	Tortworth	80 ft × 5 ft 6 in
Second only to original at Dawyck			
Fraxinus excelsior	Ash	Williamstrip	75 ft × 16 ft 9 in
Unusually big bole			
Liriodendron tulipifera	Tulip-tree	Stanway	102 ft × 15 ft 7 in
Nothofagus obliqua Roblé	Chilean beech	Tortworth	83 ft × 7 ft 1 in
Nothofagus procera Raoul	Chilean beech	Westonbirt	80 ft × 6 ft 2 in
Paulownia tomentosa	Paulownia*	Westonbirt	over 80 ft × 3 ft @ 4 ft 3 in
Incomparably largest and finest in the country			
Populus robusta	(Hybrid) Poplar	Tortworth	133 ft × 9 ft 8 in
Pterocarya × rehderiana	Hybrid wing-nut	Westonbirt	63 ft × 10 ft 0 in
Probably original, planted 1908. Biggest girth yet			
Quercus conferta	Hungarian oak	Westonbirt Park	70 ft × 11 ft 3 in
One of three biggest known		Tortworth	80 ft × 10 ft 8 in
First probably original, planted 1846.			
Quercus dentata	A Japanese oak	Westonbirt Park	50 ft × 3 ft 10 in
Tallest of this huge-leafed tree known			
Quercus kelloggii		Tortworth	80 ft × 8 ft 9 in
Only big tree of this oak known			
Quercus × leana	Lea's hybrid oak	Westonbirt	63 ft × 5 ft 4 in
Quercus imbricaria	Shingle oak	Tortworth	84 ft × 6 ft 7 in
Biggest known			
Quercus macranthera	A Caucasian oak	Westonbirt	60 ft × 7 ft 1 in
Biggest known			
Quercus palustris	Pin oak	Tortworth	80 ft × 7 ft 10 in
Quercus robur	Newland oak	Coleford	Collapsed to about 28 ft
Has been 44 ft 8 in—probable age 900–1,100. Oldest estimated oak			
Quercus trojana	Macedonian oak	Batsford	70 ft × 7 ft 9 in
Easily biggest and finest known			
Quercus velutina	Black oak	Batsford	76 ft × 8 ft 0 in
Planted 1900. Finest young specimen			
Tilia americana	American lime	Westonbirt	70 ft × 5 ft 0 in
Tallest known			
Ulmus carpinifolia	Smooth-leaved elm	Lay-by on A433 3–4 miles	80 ft × 21 ft 0 in
	Among biggest known	south-west of Cirencester	
Ulmus × hollandica vegeta	Huntingdon elm	Knockdown House,	110 ft × 12 ft 9 in
Two of avenue, planted 1843. Remarkable group,		Willesley, Tetbury	108 ft × 13 ft 10 in
as tall as any found.			

Dutch elms with them to 100 ft

Ulmus procera	English elm	Williamstrip Park	105 ft × 22 ft 0 in
Among biggest three known. Several more there, nearly as big			

* The genus *Paulownia* was named after Anna Paulownia, Princess of the Netherlands, 1795–1865.

Index

Abbotswood, *see* Swell
Ablington Manor, *see* p. 31
Acton Hall, *see* Hamfallow
Adey, More, *see* Wotton-under-Edge
Alfred's Hall, *see* p. 34
Alkerton Grange, *see* Eastington
Anderson, Ellery, *see* Shipton Sollars
Aragon, Katharine of, *see* p. 39
Arboreta, *see* pp. 40-1 and 130-1
Archer, Fred, *see* Prestbury
Arlingham, *see* p. 39
Arlington Mill, *see* pp. 27, 31 and Bibury
Arlington Row, *see* Bibury
Armada, Spanish, *see* p. 16
Arno's Court, *see* p. 129
Arts and Crafts Movement, *see* Chalford, Duntisbourne Rouse, Kempley, Oakridge and Sapperton
Ashbee, C. R., *see* Chipping Campden and Saintbury
Atkyns, Sir Robert, *see* p. 36, Duntisbourne Rouse, Sapperton and Westbury-on-Severn
Atomic Power Station, *see* Berkeley
Augustinians, *see* Lanthony Priory and p. 121
Austen, Jane, *see* Adlestrop
Avenis Farm, *see* Bisley
Avon, River, *see* Hanham Abbots, Tetbury and pp. 121 and 129

Bacon, J., *see* Sherborne
Badminton, *see* pp. 31, 41 and Great Badminton
Baker, Charles, *see* Stroud
Baker, Thomas, *see* Bisley
Baldwin, Samuel, *see* p. 36, Avening and Gloucester
Banks Fee, *see* Longborough
Barnsley brothers, *see* pp. 31, 34 and Charlton Kings, Duntisbourne Abbots, Rodmarton and Sapperton
Barnsley Park, *see* p. 32 and Barnsley
Barnsley and Jewson, *see* Coates
Barrie, Sir James, *see* Stanway
Barrington, *see* p. 32
Barton, *see* Temple Guiting
Basevi, George, *see* Minchinhampton and Painswick
Bathurst, Earl and Countess, *see* pp. 27, 34, 37, 41 and Sapperton
Batsford Park, *see* p. 41
Battlefields, *see* Cold Ashton
Beaufort, Duke and Duchess of, *see* pp. 36, 37, Shipton Moyne and Stoke Gifford
Beaufort Hunt, *see* Tetbury
Belas Knap, *see* p. 9
Belcher, Sir John, *see* Stowell
bells, *see* p. 39
Benedictines, *see* Winchcombe
Bennier, Peter, *see* Dumbleton

Bentham Manor, *see* Badgeworth
Berkeley brasses, *see* Wotton-under-Edge
Berkeley Castle, *see* pp. 16, 18, 36, Gloucester, Hamfallow and p. 121
Berkeley, Earl of, *see* pp. 9, 18, Cam, Hamfallow, Stoke Gifford and p. 121
Berkeley Knight, *see* Coberley
Berkeley Vale, *see* Alderley, Frampton-on-Severn, Ham and Stone, Hamfallow, Hinton and p. 121
Berry Hill, *see* West Dean
Betjeman, Sir John, *see* p. 121
Bewsey, J. C. N., *see* Drybrook and Stroud
Biblia Pauperum, *see* Fairford
Bibury race-course, *see* Aldsworth
Birdland, *see* Bourton-on-the-Water
Birdlip Hill, *see* p. 9 and Great Witcombe
Bixhead Quarries, *see* p. 16
Black Death, *see* p. 22
Black Friars, *see* Gloucester
Blacking, W. H. Randoll, *see* Daglingworth and Dursley
Blackleech, Alderman, *see* p. 36 and Gloucester
Blaise Castle House, *see* p. 129
Blathwayt, William, *see* p. 32 and Dyrham
Blore, Edward, *see* Cinderford
Blow, Detmar, *see* p. 31 Brookthorpe, Harescombe and Stanway
Bodley, G. F., *see* pp. 13, 33, 34, Bussage, Cainscross, France Lynch, King's Stanley, Leonard Stanley, Selsley and p. 129
Bondend, *see* Upton St. Leonards
Boteler, Sir Ralph, *see* Winchcombe
Botetourt, Lord, *see* Stoke Gifford
Bouthrop, *see* Eastleach
Bowden Hall, *see* Upton St. Leonards
Brandon, David, *see* Colesbourne
Brass Nails, the, *see* p. 125
Breadstone, *see* Hamfallow
Bridges, Mrs, *see* p. 36
Brighton Pavilion, *see* p. 32 and Sezincote
Brislington, *see* p. 129
Bristol Aeroplane Co., *see* Filton
British Museum, *see* Bibury
Broad Campden, *see* Chipping Campden
Brockweir, *see* Hewelsfield
Brown, Capability, *see* p. 41, Dodington and Whitminster
Brown, Ford Madox, *see* Selsley
Brownshill Court, *see* p. 32
Brunel, I., *see* Kemble and pp. 121 and 129
Bryans, Herbert, *see* Abenhall and Minchinhampton
Brydges, family, *see* p. 39
Brydges, Henry, *see* p. 36
Buchan, John, *see* p. 31

Buckingham, Duke of, *see* Eastington and Thornbury
Bucknall, Benjamin, *see* p. 33 and Woodchester
"Buildings of England", Penguin, *Gloucestershire*, *see* Gloucester and Tewkesbury
Bulls Cross, *see* Painswick
Burges, William, *see* p. 33 and Minchinhampton
Burlington, Lord, *see* p. 32 and Blockley
Burlison and Grylls, *see* p. 40 and Dursley
Burman, Thomas, *see* Ebrington and Sherborne
Burne-Jones, *see* Duntisbourne Abbots and Selsley
Busby of Brighton, *see* p. 125
Butlin, Billy, *see* Leonard Stanley
Butterfield, William, *see* p. 32, Driffield, Poulton, Westerleigh and Wick

Cabot, *see* p. 128
Cachemaille-Day, *see* Gloucester
Caen, nuns of, *see* Duntisbourne Rouse
Cambridge, Richard, *see* Whitminster
Campden Guild of Handicraft, *see* Saintbury
Campden Trust, *see* pp. 27, 34 and Chipping Campden
Campden, Viscount and Viscountess, *see* p. 36 and Chipping Campden
Canals, *see* p. 34, Coates, Framilode, Frampton-on-Severn, Gloucester, Lanthony Priory, Hinton, Sapperton, Stroud and Whitminster
Canford Cemetery, *see* p. 129
Cannop Ponds, *see* p. 13
Cardonell, Mary de, *see* p. 32
Cassey, Sir John, *see* Deerhurst
Castles, *see* pp. 16, 18, Berkeley, Beverston, Brimpsfield and Gloucester
Catswood, *see* Bisley
Chandos, Duke of, *see* p. 32
Chandos, Lords, *see* p. 39
Chantry, Sir Francis, *see* Alderley
Charles I, *see* Matson
Chaucer, *see* Kempsford
Chavenage, *see* Horsley
Chosen Hill, *see* Churchdown
Christmas Steps, *see* p. 128
Churchdown, *see* p. 9
Churchill, Sir Winston, *see* Standish
Churn, River, *see* p. 13, Daglingworth and Duntisbourne Leer
Cider with Rosie, *see* Slad
Cirencester, *see* pp. 24, 27, and 39
Cirencester Park, *see* pp. 27, 34 and 41
Cistercians, *see* Flaxley and Hailes
Civil War, *see* Cheltenham and Chipping Campden
Clarence, Duke and Duchess of, *see* Tewkesbury

Clayton and Bell, *see* p. 40, Avening, Barnwood, Bisley, Daylesford, Hampnett and Swell
Cleeve Common, *see* p. 9
Cleeve Hill, *see* Prestbury and Southam
Clifton, *see* p. 129
Close, Francis, *see* Cheltenham
cloth, *see* pp. 13, 19, 22, 24, 27, 29, Bibury, Bisley, Cam, Cirencester, Minchinhampton, Stroud, Tewkesbury, Uley, Woodchester and Wotton-under-Edge
Clutton, Henry, *see* p. 33 and Hatherop
Coade stone, *see* Daylesford
coal, *see* pp. 13 and 16
Coalpit Heath, *see* Westerleigh
Cobbett, William, *see* pp. 9 and 13
Cockerell, C. and R., *see* Condicote and Longborough, p. 125
Cockerell, Sir Charles, *see* p. 32 and Sezincote
Cockerell, S. P., *see* p. 32, Daylesford and Sezincote
Codrington, Bethell, *see* p. 32 and Dodington
Coleraine, Lord, *see* Driffield
Collins, Ann, *see* King's Stanley
Coln, River, *see* pp. 13, 31, Ablington, Coln St. Dennis, Quenington and Winson
Colston, Edward, *see* p. 125
Comper, Sir Ninian, *see* p. 40, Eastington, Rangeworthy, Stanton, Westonbirt with Lasborough
Concorde, the, *see* p. 39, Fairford and Filton
Conway, Lord, *see* p. 32 and Dowdeswell
Corinium Museum, *see* Cirencester
Coscombe, *see* Guiting Power
Cotswold Farm, *see* Duntisbourne Abbots
Cotswold scarp, *see* pp. 9, 19, Aston Subedge, Brookthorpe, Saintbury, Southam, Sudeley Castle and Uley
Cotswold sheep, *see* Aldsworth
Cotswold Village, A, *see* p. 31, Ablington and Bibury
Cotswold wool towns, *see* Chipping Campden and Cirencester
Cottage Improvement Society, *see* Woodchester
Court Farm, *see* Nympsfield
Coxwell, John, *see* Ablington
Crecy, Battle of, *see* p. 39, Coberley and Gloucester
Croome, William Iveson, *see* North Cerney
Crystal Palace, *see* Coates
Cumberland Basin, *see* p. 129

Daneway House, *see* Sapperton
Daniell, Thomas, *see* p. 32 and Sezincote
Daukes, S. W., *see* Cheltenham and Falfield
Daw of Berkeley, *see* Cromhall
Dawber, Guy, *see* p. 34, Broadwell and Hartpury
Daylesford House, *see* p. 32

Dean, Forest of, *see* pp. 9, 13, 16, 19, Abenhall, Blaisdon, Cinderford, Hewelsfield, Little Dean, Mitcheldean, Newland, Ruardean, Staunton (by Monmouth), Tidenham, West Dean and Woolaston
de Clare family, *see* p. 39
de la Bere family, *see* p. 36
Deerhurst, *see* p. 19
Dent family, *see* Sudeley Castle
Despencer family, *see* pp. 34, 39 and Tewkesbury
Dikler, River, *see* Little Rissington and Swell
Dixton Manor, *see* Alderton
Dodington, *see* p. 32
Domesday, *see* p. 31, Bibury, Cheltenham and Gloucester
Dominicans, *see* Gloucester
Dover's Games, *see* Aston-Subedge
Dover's Hill, *see* p. 9 and Aston-Subedge
Dowty Works, *see* Staverton
Drake, Sir Francis, *see* Awre
Dubunni, the, *see* Bagendon
Ducie Cultivator, *see* p. 41
Ducie, Earl of, *see* pp. 32, 40-1, and Tortworth
Dunraven, Countess of, *see* p. 33
Dutton, Sir John, *see* p. 37
Dutton, John, *see* Cheltenham
Dykes-Bower, Stephen, *see* Eastington
Dyrham, *see* p. 32

Earp, Thomas, *see* Huntley
East India Co., *see* p. 32
Eastleach Martin, *see* Eastleach
Eastleach Turville, *see* Eastleach
Eastwood Park, *see* Falfield
Ebley, *see* Cainscross
Eden, F. C., *see* p. 40, Ampney St. Mary, Eastington, Iron Acton, Minchinhampton, North Cerney
Edney, William, *see* Elmore
Edward the Confessor, *see* Cheltenham
Edward II, *see* pp. 18, 34, Berkeley, Brimpsfield, Cam and Gloucester
Edward IV, *see* Tewkesbury
Ellacombe family, *see* Bitton
Ellacombe, Rev. H. T., *see* Hanham Abbots
Ellenborough, Lord, *see* Southam
Elwes, Henry, *see* p. 40 and Colesbourne
Ermine Street, *see* Brimpsfield
Estcourt family, *see* Long Newnton
Estcourt Park, *see* Long Newnton
Evans, Charles, *see* p. 121
Evans, David, *see* p. 40
Evenlode, the, *see* Westcote
Everard, Edward, *see* p. 125
Evesham Vale, *see* Aston-Subedge
Ewen, *see* Kemble

Fairford, *see* p. 39
Fécamp, Abbey of, *see* Cheltenham
Fedden, Bryant, *see* Alderley and Cromhall
Ferrers, William, *see* Ashchurch
Ferrey, Benjamin, *see* Lower Slaughter
Ferris Court, *see* Bisley

Fisher, Alexander, *see* Stanway
Fitzhamon, Robert, *see* Tewkesbury
Fitzharding, Robert, *see* p. 121
FitzRoy, Robert, *see* Tewkesbury
Flaxman, John, *see* Gloucester
Flower, Barnard, *see* pp. 27, 39 and Fairford
Forbes, John, *see* Cheltenham
Ford, *see* Temple Guiting
Forester of Fee, *see* Newland
Forest House, *see* Coleford
Forestry Commission, *see* p. 13
Fortey, John, *see* p. 29
Forthampton Court, *see* p. 16
Fosse Way, *see* p. 18
Foster, James, *see* Kingswood
Frampton, Bishop, *see* Standish
Frampton Court, *see* pp. 16 and 121 and Frampton-on-Severn
Freeman Fox and Partners, *see* Aust
Freeminers, *see* p. 16
Frocester Hill, *see* p. 9
Frome, River, *see* Eastington, Sapperton, Stroud and Whitminster
Fromebridge Mill, *see* Frampton-on-Severn
Frost, Robert, *see* Dymock
Fulljames and Waller, Messrs., *see* Down Hatherley
Fulljames, Thomas, *see* Hasfield

Gambier-Parry family, *see* p. 41
Gambier-Parry, Sidney, *see* Quedgeley
Gambier-Parry, Thomas, *see* p. 33 and Highnam
Gatcombe, *see* Awre
Gatcombe Park, *see* Minchinhampton
Gaunt, John of, *see* Kempsford
Gaunt's Earthcott, *see* Almondsbury
George and Peto, *see* Batsford
George, Sir Ernest, *see* pp. 34, 41, Edgeworth and Moreton-in-Marsh
Gibbons, Grinling, *see* p. 36 and Great Badminton
Gibbs, Alexander, *see* p. 32 and Driffield
Gibbs, Arthur, *see* p. 31, Ablington and Bibury
Giffard family, *see* Brimpsfield
Gill, Eric, *see* p. 129, Ebrington and Stanway
Gimson, Ernest, *see* pp. 31, 34, Bisley, Duntisbourne Rouse, Kempley and Sapperton
Glasgow Art School, *see* p. 128
glass, stained, *see* pp. 39-40
Gloucester-Berkeley Canal, *see* p. 34, Gloucester, Lanthony Priory and Whitminster
Gloucester Cathedral, *see* p. 22
Gloucester Vale, *see* Elmore and Harescombe
Golden Valley, *see* p. 13 and Chalford
Goodhart-Rendel, H., *see* p. 33 and Batsford
Granville, Sir Bevil, *see* Cold Ashton
Green, Samuel, *see* Barnsley
Grevel, William, *see* p. 29 and Chipping Campden
Grey Friars, *see* Gloucester

Griggs, F. L., *see* pp. 27, 31, Chipping Campden and Owlpen
Grove, The, *see* Barrington
Guildo of Hereford, *see* p. 36 and Sapperton
Guise family, *see* Elmore
Guiting Grange, *see* Guiting Power
Guiting Stone, *see* p. 13 and Guiting Power

Hailes Abbey, *see* Teddington
Hale family, *see* Alderley
Halfpenny, William, *see* Frampton-on-Severn and pp. 125, 129
Hamswell, *see* Cold Ashton
Hanbury-Tracy, Charles, *see* p. 33 and Toddington
Handicrafts, Guild of, *see* Chipping Campden and p. 34
Hanham Court, *see* Hanham Abbots
Hansom, Charles, *see* p. 33, Nympsfield, Woodchester and p. 129
Harcourt-Masters, C., *see* Cold Ashton
Hardman, John, *see* pp. 39, 40 and Barnwood
Hardwick, P. C., *see* Rendcomb
Hardwicke Court, *see* p. 16
Hardy, Captain, *see* Cheltenham
Hare, Richard, *see* Gloucester
Haresfield Beacon, *see* p. 9
Harrington House, *see* Bourton-on-the-Water
Harris, Vincent, *see* p. 128
Hastings, Warren, *see* p. 32 and Daylesford
Hatherly Court, *see* Down Hatherley
Hatherop Castle, *see* p. 33
Hauduroy, Samuel, *see* Dyrham
Haw Bridge, *see* Tirley
Hawkesbury Upton, *see* Hawkesbury
Hayward, John, *see* Mitcheldean
Hazle House, *see* Miserden
Heaton, Butler and Bayne, *see* p. 40
Henbury, *see* p. 129
Hendly, Robert, *see* Aldsworth
Henriques, Robert, *see* p. 31
Henry VIII, *see* p. 36, Gloucester and Sudeley Castle
Hertford, Earl of, *see* p. 32
Hetty Pegler's Tump, *see* p. 9 and Uley
Hicks, Sir Baptist, *see* p. 29 and Chipping Campden
Hicks-Beach, Sir Michael, *see* Coln St. Aldwyns
Highnam, *see* p. 41
Hill, Oliver, *see* Long Newnton
Hilles, *see* Harescombe
Hinchwick Manor, *see* Condicote
Hiorn, Francis, *see* Tetbury
Holden, Charles, *see* p. 128
Holford, Robert, *see* p. 40
Hooper, Bishop, *see* Ashchurch, Cranham and Gloucester
Horse Trials, *see* Great Badminton
Horsnaile, Christopher, *see* Dowdeswell
Hotwells Spa, *see* p. 129
Howard, F. E., *see* Bourton-on-the-Water
Humphreys End, *see* Randwick

Hungerford family, *see* Down Ampney
Huntingdon, Chapel of Countess of, *see* Gotherington
Huntley family, *see* Boxwell
Huntley Manor, *see* p. 41
Huxley, Professor, *see* p. 34

Industrial Revolution, *see* p. 27 and Wotton-under-Edge
Inglesham, *see* Lechlade
Isbourne, River, *see* Winchcombe

Jackson, Sir T. G., *see* Bourton-on-the-Water, Dursley and Iron Acton
Jaynes Court, *see* Bisley
Jearrad, R. W. and C., *see* Cheltenham
Jellicoe, Geoffrey, *see* Cheltenham
Jenner, Dr., *see* p. 37
Jenner's Hut, *see* Berkeley
Jewson, Norman, *see* p. 34
Johnson, Thomas of Warwick, *see* Aston-Subedge
Johnston, Lawrence, *see* Hidcote and p. 41

Keble House, *see* Fairford
Keble, John, *see* Coln St. Aldwyns and Eastleach
Keble, Thomas, *see* Bisley and Southrop
Kebles, the, *see* Stinchcombe
Keck, Anthony, *see* Flaxley
Kelmscott, *see* Lechlade
Kempe, C. E., *see* p. 40, Bourton-on-the-Water, Bromsberrow, and Colesbourne
Kempson of Hereford, *see* Blaisdon
Kent, William, *see* pp. 31-2, 34, Barrington and Great Badminton
Key, Thomas, *see* Cold Ashton
Keyt, Sir John and Lady, *see* Ebrington
Kidderminster, Abbot Richard, *see* Winchcombe
Kineton, *see* Temple Guiting
King of Bath, *see* Cromhall
King, Thomas, *see* p. 37
King's College Chapel, Cambridge, *see* Fairford
Kings Weston House, *see* p. 129
Kingscote family, *see* Kingscote
Kingsdown, *see* pp. 128-9
Kip, *see* Westbury-on-Severn
Knight and Chatters, *see* Alderton
Knight, W. H., *see* Cheltenham and Prestbury
Knole Park, *see* Almondsbury

Lammas Park, *see* Minchinhampton
Landsdown Hill, *see* p. 9
Lansdown, Battle of, *see* Cold Ashton
Lansdown, Cheltenham, *see* Cheltenham
Lanthony, Prior of, *see* Brockworth
Lanthony Priory, *see* Gloucester
Lasborough Manor, *see* Westonbirt with Lasborough
Lasborough Park, *see* Westonbirt with Lasborough
Laud, William, *see* Gloucester
Leach, River, *see* p. 13
Leckhampton stone, *see* Cheltenham

Lee, Laurie, *see* Slad
Leigh, Sir William, *see* Longborough
Leigh, William, *see* p. 33
Leigh, Theophilus, *see* Adlestrop
Leland, *see* p. 13
limestone, *see* p. 9
Llandoger Trow, *see* p. 125
Lloyd family, *see* p. 36
London, George, *see* Dyrham
Lowbands, *see* Staunton (by Newent)
Lower Througham, *see* Bisley
Luffinghams, *see* Fretherne with Saul
Lutyens, Sir Edwin, *see* Miserden, Stonehouse, Swell and Upper Slaughter
Lyegrove House, *see* Sodbury
Lysons family, *see* Hempsted

Macintosh, Hugh, *see* p. 128
Marshall, Joshua, *see* p. 36 and Chipping Campden
Master, Dr., *see* Cirencester
Master, Sir Thomas, *see* p. 36
Matilda, Queen, *see* Tewkesbury
Mauley, Lord and Lady de, *see* p. 39 and Hatherop
May Hill, *see* Taynton
Mazer bowl, *see* Buckland
Mears, Thomas, *see* p. 39
Medford House, *see* Mickleton
Medland, James, *see* Tibberton
Medland-Maberly, *see* p. 33
Merchant Venturers Almshouses, *see* p. 125
Messel, Oliver, *see* Flaxley
Middle Lypiatt, *see* Bisley
Middleton, John, *see* p. 33, Charlton Kings, Cheltenham, Clearwell, Coberley and Oxenhall
Miller, Sanderson, *see* Adlestrop and Siston
Minchinhampton Common, *see* p. 9 and Amberley
minerals, *see* pp. 13 and 16
Miss Mackenzie, *see* Cheltenham
Mitchell, Alan, *see* p. 9
Monti, Raffaelle, *see* p. 39 and Hatherop
Montpellier, *see* Cheltenham
Moore, Temple, *see* Great Badminton and Stroud
More Hall, *see* Randwick
Morris, William, *see* pp. 31, 34, 40, Bibury, Lechlade and Selsley
Motorway Crossing, *see* Almondsbury
Mott, Hay and Anderson, *see* Aust
Mylne, Robert, *see* p. 34, Hinton and Quedgeley
Mylne and Telford, *see* Gloucester
Mushet, David, *see* Coleford, Staunton (by Monmouth)

Nailsworth, *see* p. 13 and Horsley
Nash, John, *see* Barnsley and p. 129
National Gallery, *see* p. 39
National Trust, *see* p. 9, Bibury, Dyrham, Hailes, Haresfield, Hidcote, Snowshill, Westbury-on-Severn and p. 41 and p. 129
Nelson, Lord, *see* Cheltenham
Nether Lypiatt Manor, *see* Bisley

Newark Park, *see* Ozleworth
Newton, Sir Isaac, *see* Barnsley
Niblett, Francis, *see* Framilode and Fretherne with Saul
Nibley House, *see* North Nibley
Nollekens, Joseph, *see* Arlingham
Norman Conquest, *see* p. 19
Norman remains, *see* pp. 19, 21, Dymock, Eastleach, Edgeworth, Elkstone, Hampnett, Notgrove, Oxenhall, Ozleworth, Pauntley, Quenington, Rangeworthy, Rendcomb, Radford, St. Briavels, Siddington, Swindon, Syde, Windrush, and Yanworth
Normandy, Robert Duke of, *see* p. 36
North Cotswolds hounds, *see* Temple Guiting
North, Marianne, *see* Alderley
Northumberland, Earl of, *see* p. 9
Northwick Park, *see* pp. 32, 37 and Blockley
Norton, John, *see* Frampton Cotterell and p. 129

Oatley, Sir George, *see* p. 125
O'Connor, Feargus, *see* Corse
Odda, Earl, *see* Deerhurst
Odda's Chapel, *see* Deerhurst
Offa's Dyke, *see* p. 13
Onley, Samuel, *see* pp. 9 and 13
Oolite stone, *see* pp. 9 and 13
Opus Anglicanum, *see* Baunton, Buckland, and Chipping Campden
Orcagna, *see* p. 39
Oriel Lodge, *see* Cheltenham
Osney, Abbey of, *see* p. 31, Aldsworth and Bibury
Owlpen Manor, *see* p. 31
Oxford Movement, *see* Southrop

Pace, Richard, *see* Lechlade
Painswick Beacon, *see* pp. 9 and 31
Painswick House, *see* p. 121
Painswick masons, *see* p. 36
Painswick stone, *see* p. 36 and Elmore
Papworth, John, *see* Cheltenham
Parkend, *see* West Dean
Parr, Katharine, *see* p. 37
Patchway, *see* Almondsbury
Paterson, Robert, *see* p. 41
Paty family, *see* p. 37, Cromhall, pp. 121, 125 and 129
Paul, Sir Onesiphorus, *see* p. 37 and Little Dean
Pauncefoote family, *see* Hasfield
Payne, Henry, *see* p. 40
Pearce, J., of Frampton, *see* p. 37, Frampton-on-Severn, Ham and Stone, and Longney
Pearson, J. L., *see* Daylesford, North Nibley, Stinchcombe and p. 128
Pennant stone, *see* Doynton, Mangotsfield and Westerleigh
Penrose, F. C., *see* Apperley
Pepys, Samuel, *see* Standish
Perrot, Henry, *see* p. 32
Philip, J. Birnie, *see* p. 37, Flaxley and Sudeley Castle
Pinbury Park, *see* p. 31 and Duntisbourne Rouse

Pitchcombe House, *see* p. 32
Pitman, Isaac, *see* Wotton-under-Edge
Pitt, Joseph, *see* Cheltenham
Ponting, C. E., *see* Almondsbury and Down Ampney
Poole, Sir Henry, *see* p. 36
Pope, Alexander, *see* pp. 27, 31, 41 and Bibury
Porter, Endymion, *see* Aston-Subedge
Potter, Robert, *see* Gloucester
Powell, Alfred, *see* p. 31
Powell's glass, *see* p. 40
prehistoric remains, *see* p. 9, Ablington, Bagendon, Cheltenham and Uley
"Present State of Gloucestershire", *see* Westbury-on-Severn
Prevost, Sir George, *see* Stinchcombe
Prichard of Llandaff, *see* Chipping Campden
Prinknash Abbey, *see* pp. 31, 39 and Upton St. Leonards
Prothero, H. A., *see* Cheltenham
Pugin, A. W. N., *see* p. 33
Pulham, James, *see* p. 41
Purton, *see* Hinton
Pyrke family, *see* Abenhall

Rack Isle, *see* Bibury
Ragged Castle, *see* p. 34
Red Bridge, *see* Quedgeley
Red Lodge, *see* p. 121
Redesdale, Lord, *see* pp. 34, 41 and Batsford
Redland, *see* p. 129
Regent, Prince, *see* Cheltenham
Reinbald, *see* Cheltenham
Rendcomb, *see* p. 39
Repton, George S., *see* Dumbleton
Repton, Humphry, *see* p. 32 and Adlestrop
Richard III, *see* Sudeley Castle and Tewkesbury
Ricketts of Gloucester, *see* p. 37 and Upton St. Leonards
Rickman, Thomas, *see* Horsley
Ringerike style, *see* Bibury
Roberts House, *see* Siddington
Roberts, Sir Gilbert, *see* Aust
Robins Wood Hill, *see* p. 9
Robson, E. R., *see* Cheltenham
Roel Farm, *see* Hawling
Rogers, George of Worcester, *see* p. 40 and Barnwood and Fretherne with Saul
Rogers, William, *see* Dowdeswell
Rolls-Royce, *see* Filton
Roman remains, *see* pp. 9, 18-19, Barnsley, Cheltenham, Cirencester, Lydney and p. 121
Roman villas, *see* p. 19, Barnsley, Bisley, Chedworth, Cirencester, Frocester, Great Witcombe and Woodchester
Rosehill, *see* Cheltenham
Rosehill School, *see* Alderley
Rossetti, D. G., *see* Selsley
Royal Agricultural College, *see* p. 27 and Cirencester
Royal Fort, *see* p. 121

Rudhall, Abraham, *see* p. 39 and Colesbourne
Rudhall, Thomas, *see* Baunton
Rupert, Prince, *see* Aston-Subedge
Rushout, Sir John, *see* p. 32
Ruskin, John, *see* France Lynch
Rysbrack, *see* p. 37, Blockley, Great Badminton, Sherborne and pp. 125, 128

Sackville-West, V., *see* p. 18 and p. 41
Sally-on-the-Barn, *see* Hanham Abbots
Salvin, Anthony, *see* Thornbury
sandstone, *see* p. 9, Abenhall and Bulley
Sandys monument, *see* p. 36
Sandywell Park, *see* p. 32 and Dowdeswell
Saunders, Samuel, *see* Tetbury
Saxon remains, *see* pp. 16, 19, Bibury, Bitton, Cheltenham, Coln Rogers, Daglingworth, Deerhurst, Somerford Keynes, Winstone, Wormington and p. 121
Scott, Sir G. G., *see* p. 34, Ampney St. Peter, Flaxley, Gloucester, Gretton, Sudeley Castle and Winchcombe
Scott, G. G. (junior), *see* Stroud
Scott, J. R., *see* Cheltenham
Seddon, J. P., *see* Redbrook
Serlo, Abbot, *see* Gloucester
Severn Bridge, *see* p. 16 and Aust
Severn, River, *see* pp. 9, 13, 16, 18, 19, 31, Arlingham, Ashleworth, Awre, Beachley, Forthampton, Framilode, Minsterworth, Newent, Newnham-on-Severn, Norton, Tidenham and Woolaston
Severn Wild Fowl Trust, *see* p. 18 and Slimbridge
Sewell, Katheryn, *see* Bisley
Seymour, Lord, *see* Winchcombe
Sezincote, *see* p. 32 and Daylesford
Sharpness, *see* Hinton
Shaw, Norman, *see* Almondsbury
Shelley, P. B., *see* Lechlade
Sherborne, Lord, *see* Standish
Shingler, Risdon and Associates, *see* Gloucester
Shirehampton, *see* p. 129
Siddington, *see* p. 39
Sievier, R. W., *see* p. 37
Sitwell, Sacheverell, *see* Bisley
Smirke, Sir Robert, *see* p. 125, Gloucester and Hardwicke
Snell, Sir Thomas, *see* p. 37
Snig's End, *see* Corse and Staunton (by Newent)
Soane, Sir John, *see* Cheltenham and Down Ampney
Solomon's Court, *see* Bisley
Somers-Clarke, George, *see* Cowley
Somerset, Lord Rupert, *see* Hawkesbury
Soudley, *see* Cinderford
Southfield Mill House, *see* Woodchester
Speech House, *see* p. 41 and West Dean
St. Aldwyn, Lord, *see* Coln St. Aldwyns

St. Briavels Castle, *see* St. Briavels and West Dean
Stammers, H., *see* p. 40 and Sandhurst
Stancombe Park, *see* Stinchcombe
Stanley Mills, *see* King's Stanley
Stanton Court, *see* p. 31
Stanway House, *see* pp. 13, 31 and 41
Stapleton, *see* p. 129
Stinchcombe Hill, *see* p. 9
Stocking, William, *see* p. 121
Stoke Bishop, *see* p. 129
Stoke Park, *see* Stoke Gifford
stone, *see* Coade, Guiting, Painswick, Oolite, Pennant, limestone, Leckhampton and sandstone
Stone, *see* Ham and Stone
Stone, Nicholas, *see* p. 36
Stott, Sir Philip, *see* Stanton
Stowell Park, *see* Yanworth
Strahan, John, *see* Frampton-on-Severn and p. 121
Stratford family, *see* p. 36
Stratton-Davis, David, *see* Churchdown
Street Farm, *see* Nympsfield
Street, G. E., *see* pp. 13, 33, Kempsford, Prestbury, Sodbury, Toddington, Whelford, Winterbourne and p. 128
Stroud valleys, *see* pp. 13 and 31
Stroudwater canal, *see* p. 34 and Framilode
Sudeley Castle, *see* p. 39 and Winchcombe
Sudeley, Lord, *see* p. 33
Suspension Bridge, *see* p. 121
Swan Cottages, *see* p. 31 and Bibury
Sydenhams, *see* Bisley
Symond's Yat, *see* pp. 13 and 16
Syon, Abbess of, *see* Cheltenham and Duntisbourne Rouse

Talbot, Earl, *see* p. 32
Talman, *see* p. 32 and Dyrham
Tanner Chapel, *see* Dursley
Telford, Thomas, *see* p. 34 and Hinton
Temple Meads station, *see* p. 129
Tetbury Upton House, *see* p. 121
Teulon, S. S., *see* pp. 32, 40, Huntley, Kingscote, Newington Bagpath, North Nibley, Nympsfield, Tortworth, Uley and Woodchester
Thames, *see* p. 19, Ampney Crucis, Down Ampney, Lechlade, Shorncote, Somerford Keynes, South Cerney and Tetbury
Thames-Severn canal, *see* p. 34 and Coates and Sapperton
Thomas, Edward, *see* Adlestrop
Thompson, Pearson, *see* Cheltenham
Thornbury Castle, *see* p. 16, Littleton-upon-Severn and Thornbury
Throckmorton, Thomas, *see* p. 36
Througham Slad, *see* Bisley
Tinling, Canon, *see* p. 39 and Gloucester
Tortworth, *see* pp. 40-1
Tower, Walter, *see* Redbrook

Tractarian times, *see* Ampney Crucis and Barnsley
Trinity Mill, *see* Bagendon
Trollope, Anthony, *see* Cheltenham
Trye family, *see* p. 30
Tutshill, *see* Tidenham
tympana, *see* p. 21
Tyndale monument, *see* North Nibley
Tyndale, William, *see* Little Sodbury

Under-the-Hill House, *see* Wotton-under-Edge
Underwood, G. A., *see* Cheltenham
Upper Soudley Ponds, *see* p. 13

Vanbrugh, Sir John, *see* p. 129
Vaughan-Williams, Dr. Ralph, *see* Down Ampney
Veele, Edward, *see* p. 36
Victoria & Albert Museum, *see* Wotton-under-Edge
Viollet-le-Duc, Eugene, *see* p. 33 and Woodchester
Vulliamy, Lewis, *see* pp. 33, 40, Alderley, Beverston, Hawkesbury, Highnam, Tetbury, Westonbirt with Lasborough

Waals, Peter, *see* p. 31
Wailes, William, *see* p. 40, Colesbourne and Stow-on-the-Wold
Wainlode Hill, *see* Norton
Wakeman, Abbot, *see* Forthampton
Waller family, *see* pp. 33-4
Wallsworth Hall, *see* Sandhurst
Wallton, Alderman, *see* p. 36
Walpole, Horace, *see* p. 31, Dowdeswell and Upton St. Leonards
Wanswell Court, *see* Hamfallow
Ware, Isaac, *see* p. 129
Watercombe, *see* Bisley
Waterhouse, Alfred, *see* p. 125
Waterlane House, *see* Bisley
Webb, Christopher, *see* Ebrington
Webb, Geoffrey, *see* p. 40 and Shipton Sollars
Webb, John, *see* Sherborne
Webb, Philip, *see* Forthampton and Selsley and p. 34
Wellington, Duke of, *see* Cheltenham
Wells, Randall, *see* Kempley
Wemyss, Countess of, *see* Stanway
Wesley, John, *see* Hanham Abbots
West, Anthony, *see* Cheltenham
Westbury Court Garden, *see* Westbury-on-Severn
Westbury-on-Trym, *see* p. 129
Westmacott, R., *see* Great Badminton and Sherborne
Westington Quarry, *see* Chipping Campden
Westonbirt, *see* pp. 33 and 40
Whall, Christopher, *see* p. 40, Avening, Bagendon and Gloucester

Whall, Veronica, *see* Barnwood
Wheeler, Sir Charles, *see* p. 128
White, Sir George, *see* Filton
White, William, *see* West Dean
Whitefield, George, *see* Hanham Abbots and Kingswood
Whiteway Colony, *see* Miserden
Whittington, Dick, *see* Notgrove and Pauntley
Whitworth, Robert, *see* p. 34
Wick Court, *see* Arlingham
Wiggin, Rev. W., *see* Hampnett
Wilde, Oscar, *see* Wotton-under-Edge
Wildfowl Trust, *see* Severn Wildfowl Trust
Willement, Thomas, *see* p. 40 and Great Badminton
William I, *see* Gloucester and Tewkesbury
William II, *see* Tewkesbury
William III, *see* p. 128
Williams, Isaac, *see* Stinchcombe
Williamstrip Park, *see* p. 41 and Coln St. Aldwyns
Wilson, Henry, *see* p. 39 and Gloucester
Wilson, J., *see* Cheltenham
Windrush, River, *see* p. 13, Barrington, Bourton-on-the-Water, Naunton and Temple Guiting
Wollaton Hall, *see* Westonbirt with Lasborough
Wood, John, the elder, *see* p. 125
Woodchester Park, *see* pp. 33 and 40
Woodchester valley, *see* Amberley
Woodforde, Christopher, *see* p. 39
Woodhouse, Violet Gordon, *see* Bisley
Woodroffe, Paul, *see* Chipping Campden
Woodward family, *see* Blockley
Woodyer, Henry, *see* pp. 32-33, Highnam, Lydrook, Minsterworth and Quedgeley
Woolfe, John, *see* p. 32 and Blockley
Woolstone Hill, *see* Alstone
Worcester, Bishop of, *see* Bishops Cleeve
Worcester Lodge, *see* p. 34 and Great Badminton
Works, Ministry of Public Building and, *see* Gloucester and Hailes
Wright, Thomas, *see* p. 34, Great Badminton and Stoke Gifford
Wyatt, James, *see* Dodington, Ozleworth, Westonbirt-with-Lasborough
Wyatt, J. D., *see* Gretton
Wyatt, T. H., *see* Acton Turville, Bisley, Didmarton, Long Newnton and Shipton Moyne
Wyatville, Sir Jeffry, *see* Bisley
Wycliffe College, *see* Stonehouse
Wye river, *see* p. 13, Lancaut and Tidenham
Wynter, Admiral, *see* Awre
Wynter, George, *see* p. 36

Yate family, *see* Arlingham

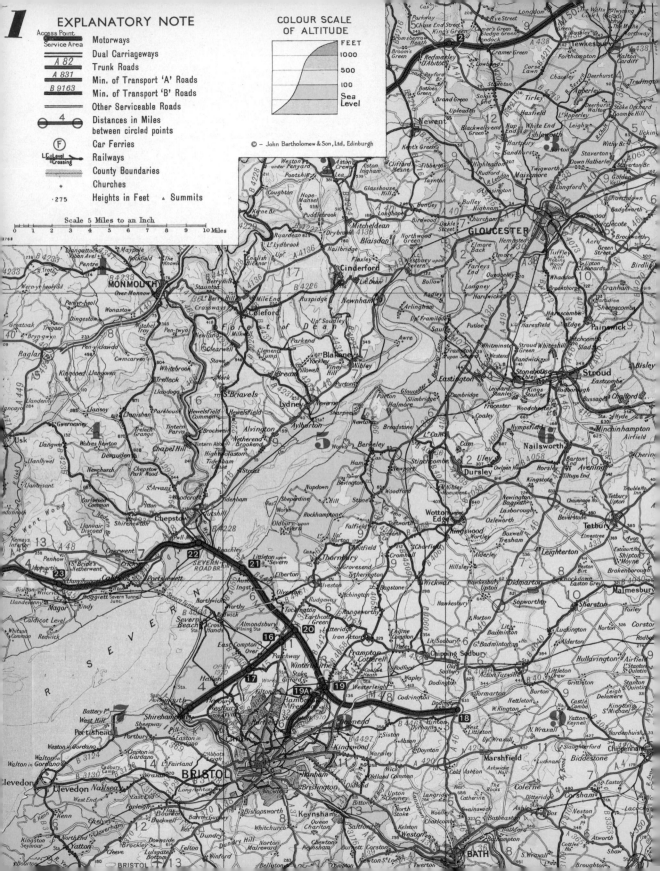

© – John Bartholomew & Son, Ltd., Edinburgh.

1

EXPLANATORY NOTE

Access Point / Service Area	Motorways
	Dual Carriageways
A 82	Trunk Roads
A 831	Min. of Transport 'A' Roads
B 9163	Min. of Transport 'B' Roads
	Other Serviceable Roads
4	Distances in Miles between circled points
F	Car Ferries
L.C. Level Crossing	Railways
	County Boundaries
+	Churches
·275	Heights in Feet ▲ Summits

COLOUR SCALE OF ALTITUDE

FEET
1000
500
100
Sea Level

Scale 5 Miles to an Inch

0 1 2 3 4 5 6 7 8 9 10 Miles

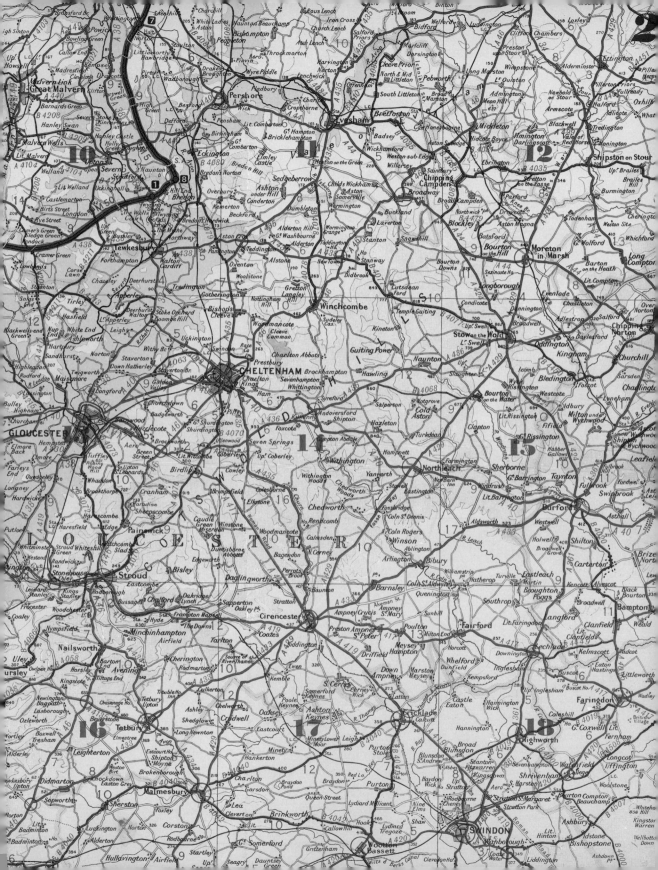